ALSO BY JAY MCINERNEY

NONFICTION

Bacchus and Me

FICTION

A Hedonist in the Cellar

A
Hedonist
in the Cellar

ADVENTURES IN WINE

Jay McInerney

ALFRED A. KNOPF, NEW YORK, 2006

THIS IS A BORZOI BOOK
PUBLISHED BY ALFRED A. KNOPF

Copyright © 2006 by Bright Lights, Big City, Inc.

All rights reserved. Published in the United States by Alfred A. Knopf,
a division of Random House, Inc., New York, and in Canada by
Random House of Canada Limited, Toronto.
www.aaknopf.com

Knopf, Borzoi Books, and the colophon are registered trademarks
of Random House, Inc.

All of the essays in this work were
originally published in *House & Garden* magazine.

Library of Congress Cataloging-in-Publication Data

McInerney, Jay.
A hedonist in the cellar : adventures in wine / Jay McInerney. —1st ed.
          p.   cm.
Includes bibliographical references.
ISBN 1-4000-4482-0
     1. Wine and wine making.   I. Title.

TP548.M4689 2006   641.2'2—dc22   2006045287

Manufactured in the United States of America
First Edition

FOR LORA

"I can certainly see you know your wine. Most of the guests who stay here wouldn't know the difference between Bordeaux and claret."

—JOHN CLEESE AS BASIL FAWLTY

CONTENTS

ix

CONTENTS

CONTENTS

xi

My careers as a novelist and as a wine writer could both plausibly be said to have their humble beginnings in the Westcott Cordial Shop in Syracuse, New York. While studying with Raymond Carver and Tobias Wolff in the Graduate Writing Program at Syracuse University, I was working behind the counter of this boozeteria, located in a marginal neighborhood a mile or two from the university campus, when I heard that my first novel had been accepted for publication by Random House. And it was there, in between working on the revisions of the novel and riding out the occasional stickup at gunpoint, that I read through the proprietor's dusty collection of wine books. A significant portion of our business was in the sale of that spirit-fortified grape juice which sustained hardcore, low-budget alcoholics: Night Train, Wild Irish Rose, MD 20/20. But we also sold some real wine—that is, grape juice that had actually undergone fermentation—and it was a tradition among the clerks to take home a bottle each night. I started with, as I recall, a two-dollar bottle of Yugoslavian Cab and worked all the way up to Freixenet, a Spanish sparkler that sold for $5.95 at the time. The owner also kept a small stock of Bordeaux and Burgundy on a shelf near the cash register, dusty bottles that had never moved during my tenure in the store. The day I heard my novel was to be published I bought one of them, a 1978 Smith-Haut-Lafitte, and while, objectively speaking, it was far from the best Bordeaux I've ever had, I don't for a minute believe that wine appreciation is a strictly objective enterprise: I've gotten far less pleasure out of more expensive and highly regarded bottles of Bordeaux in the years since.

Bad as some of the wine I was lifting from the store shelves was, it was probably an improvement, in an aesthetic and toxicological sense, from the harder stuff to which I subscribed in my early years in Manhattan. Oenophilia was a way of channeling the hedonistic impulse, of refining and intellectualizing it to some extent. Wine is an intoxicant, and we shouldn't pretend otherwise, although you might never know it on the basis of most of what's written in the wine journals. And let's face it: if it weren't, we wouldn't be drawn to it. But it can provide intellectual as well as sensual pleasure; it's an inexhaustible subject, a nexus of subjects, which leads us, if we choose to follow, into the realms of geology, botany, meteorology, history, aesthetics, and literature. Ideally, the appreciation of wine is balanced between consumption and pleasure on the one hand and contemplation and analysis on the other.

My interest in the grape has led me to some of the more beautiful parts of the world—Alsace, Tuscany, Provence, the Cape of Good Hope, the Willamette Valley, to name a few— and brought me into contact with some of the most stimulating and congenial eccentrics of our time. Wine people are as a rule gregarious, generous, and passionate. The cult of Bacchus doesn't include many anal-retentive personalities. I learned a lot about viticulture from Angelo Gaja over dinner at a trattoria in Barbaresco, but what I remember most vividly was the story of how he smashed his television set with a sledgehammer after he decided his kids were watching it too much. And I'll never forget Joan Dillon at Château Haut-Brion talking about hijinks on President Kennedy's yacht, or Allen Ginsberg disrobing in the offices of the *Paris Review.* Our love of wine is the fraternal bond that brings us together, and it is the lubricant that stimulates our conversation, but it's a polygamous relationship that encourages and enhances our other passions. It leads us to other subjects and leads us back to the world. It lifts us up and delivers us from the mundane circumstances of daily life, inspires contemplation, and, ultimately, returns us to that very world, refreshed, with enriched understanding and appreciation.

Fermented grape juice is a far more potent catalyst for contemplation and meditation than a highball, or an eight ball. It is a sacramental beverage, a sacred and symbolic liquid. "Do this in memory of me," Jesus said as he lifted a chalice of wine, and indeed wine can serve as a mnemonic device, a catalyst of memory. But that shouldn't prevent us from enjoying it unself-consciously. Wine is as serious or as frivolous as we wish to make it. Like sex, it has far too often been shrouded in mystery, hemmed in by taboo, obfuscated by technical blather, and assailed by puritans, though its enjoyment is, or should be, simple, accessible, and entertaining. Michel Chapoutier, one of the world's most serious and successful winemakers, once ordered me to stop thinking so hard about a glass of wine I was nosing. "If you think too much you kill it," he said. We were sitting on the terrace of his sprawling house at the crest of a ridge high above the Rhône River, just south of the town of Tain l'Hermitage, digesting a spectacular lunch with the aid of his '99 Hermitage *vin de paille.* "The brain is a pleasure killer," he said, before concluding with the sort of politically incorrect analogy French wine-makers seem to adore: "You don't need to be a gynecologist to make love." In Europe, where wine has been a part of daily life for thousands of years, American oenophiles are sometimes viewed as monomaniacs—zealous and somewhat narrow-minded converts to a generous and pantheistic faith. American wine lovers need to broaden their vision and relax: to see wine as just another aspect of the well-lived life.

Some ten years after my stint at the Westcott Cordial Shop—ten years ago, in fact—my friend Dominique Browning, who had just been named editor in chief of *House & Garden,* asked me if I would consider writing a wine column for the magazine. I demurred, believing that I wasn't nearly knowledge-able enough to set myself up as an authority on wine. It was true that I spent far too much time reading wine books, wine catalogs, and weather reports from Bordeaux; I sometimes bored my dinner guests with rapturous encomiums to what-ever I was serving them; and on the average night I drank more wine than my doctor would have recommended. I'd been known to jump on a plane to London if my friend Julian Barnes, who has a world-class cellar and isn't afraid to uncork his treasures, invited me to dinner. But I'd never taken a class, or attended a wine tasting, or spit into a bucket, and for the life of me I had no idea what was meant by the phrases "malo-lactic fermentation" or "volatile acidity." And I had very little knowledge of flowers or floral scents, which seemed a prereq-uisite for a certain kind of wine writing. Besides, I already had a job.

Around the time Dominique brought up the wine-column idea I was asked to write a profile of Julia Roberts, a request I initially turned down out of . . . well, I don't know what the hell it was—a sense of highbrow self-importance, I guess. "I don't do celebrity profiles," I sniffed to the editor. "Are you insane?" my agent said to me later, when I told her the story. "Somebody wants to pay you good money to hang out with Julia Roberts and you said no?" In that light, I suddenly decided that my scruples were foolish. And on second thought, the wine column seemed like a similar opportunity. A good friend was offering to pay me to indulge one of my obses-sions, and to travel to stunning places to taste wine and meet kindred spirits. It seemed like a no-brainer. Still, I was a little nervous about my scanty qualifications. So I decided to write as a passionate amateur and to employ a metaphoric lan-guage; I was more comfortable comparing wines to actresses, rock bands, pop songs, painters, or automobiles than I was with literal parsing of scents and tastes à la "bouquet of American Beauty roses." If I'd had a role model here it would have been Auberon Waugh, the son of novelist Evelyn Waugh, whom I first met at a lunch for the satirical magazine *Private Eye.* As I recall, Waugh had just published a pretty fierce parody of my latest book, but I couldn't help being charmed by him and grateful that in person he was as benign and charming as he was savage in print.

As it happens, he was friends with my oenophiliac mentor Julian Barnes, and I subsequently shared a number of bottles with him over dinners at Julian's house. As a guest he was always vague and complimentary about the wine. Not so in print. Again, I couldn't help liking him, if only because he wrote some of the sharpest and funniest wine criticism of all time, collected in a slim volume called *Waugh on Wine*.

In his essay "Perils of Being a Wine Writer," he declares, "Wine writing should be camped-up. The writer should never like a wine, he should be in love with it; never find a wine disappointing but identify it as a mortal enemy, an attempt to poison him; sulphuric acid should be discovered where there is the faintest hint of sharpness. Bizarre and improbable sidetastes should be proclaimed: mushrooms, rotting wood, black treacle, burned pencils, condensed milk, sewage, the smell of French railway stations or ladies underwear." As a wine writer I consider Waugh a forebear of sorts, although I have to admit that I am more of a lover than a killer. While I have encountered many despicable wines in the course of pursuing my duties as a wine columnist, I've written more often about those that make me drool, that make me weak in the knees, that make the hair on the back of my arms stand at attention. That make me want to howl at the moon and kiss my girlfriend repeatedly.

The title under which I hoped to write my column, "An Idiot in the Cellar," reflected my ambition to be honest about my own ignorance relative to the acumen of professional critics like Robert Parker and Jancis Robinson. Dominique quashed the title, and I suppose that now, ten years later, it would be disingenuous to pretend I haven't learned what malolactic fermentation is, or that I can't usually distinguish a Burgundy from a Bordeaux.

Anyone who drinks and tastes as often as I do is bound to have the equivalent of a fish story, a tale of a blind-tasting triumph, and mine dates back to a moment some four years ago. Watching me that night at New York's La Grenouille restaurant, a stuffy temple of the old-style haute cuisine, you might have believed I was truly an expert. I had arrived late for a dinner party thrown by a deep-pocketed friend. The other guests were already seated and had red wine in their glasses. A carafe sat on the table. "Here's Jay," my friend announced. "He knows wine. He'll guess what we're drinking." Somehow this announcement coincided with a lull in the conversational din throughout the room; it seemed to me that all eyes from the surrounding tables, in addition to those of my dinner companions, were turned on me. The sommelier, who happened to be standing nearby, handed me a glass and poured from the carafe, then stood back and smirked, while the entire restaurant, or so it seemed to me at the time, looked up at me expectantly. Unable to think of any graceful escape, I stuck my nose in the glass. "Haut-Brion," I declared, eliciting a chorus of gasps. I examined the color and took a sip. "Nineteen eighty-two," I added. From the expressions of surprise and wonder I could see that I'd scored. I sat down to bask in the general admiration, and felt that perhaps all my years of drinking and tasting and spitting and reading had not been entirely wasted. Of course, there was a story behind this story, a bit of a trick involved, as there often is, and you'll find it in the following pages in my essay on Haut-Brion.

A far more typical story, which demonstrates the precariousness of my claim to expertise, was a recent dinner that involved Haut-Brion's sister property, La Mission–Haut-Brion. I was visiting my friend Julian once again at his home in North London. My dinner partner, Jancis Robinson, the excessively modest and exceedingly attractive wine authority, had just correctly guessed that the wine we were drinking was a Bordeaux from the Graves district. "Well, it can't be La Mission," I said confidently—La Mission–Haut-Brion being among my favorite wines. "Well, it is," Julian happily informed me. So much for impressing my new girlfriend, who had never seen me in full wine wonk mode before.

As much sadomasochistic fun as I find it to be, comparing and contrasting old Bordeaux vintages is less and less a part of the job description for the postmodern wine writer, and I think my own interests and tastes reflect certain trends. I still have a lot of Bordeaux in my cellar, right up to vintage 2003, and come August I start to follow weather reports from that part of the world. Bordeaux was my first love, and it remains a kind of touchstone. But increasingly I am drawn to its rival Burgundy, the Turgenev to Bordeaux's Tolstoy, and when I'm looking for sheer power and exuberance and less finesse, to the Dostoyevskian southern Rhône. If my first collection of columns devoted inordinate space to the cult Cabernets of the Napa Valley (think Hemingway), whose emergence more or less coincided with my own career as a wine writer, it seems to me that Sonoma and Santa Barbara County Pinots (Fitz-gerald) are the new cultish reds. These wines are inspired in part by the great red wines of France's Burgundy region, and the renaissance there, driven in part by a younger generation inheriting the old domains, is another heartening develop-ment. Pinot has become a household word since its starring role in Alexander Payne's *Sideways*. Syrah, meanwhile, keeps threatening to become a Californian star, but so far its career has been a little like that of the actor Orlando Bloom, more promising than happening. Or even—Syrah being a high-testosterone grape—more like that of Colin Farrell, a putative star who has yet to produce a major hit.

France and the Napa Valley are increasingly sharing the wine lists of major restaurants and the hearts of wine lovers with other regions. Stellenbosch, Solvang, Mendoza, Priorat, and Alba are among my recent destinations. When I started the column Argentina was a joke and Spain was still emerg-ing from the shadows of the Franco era; now Argentinian Malbec, grown in the high foothills of the Andes, is a hot com-modity and Spain has probably overtaken Italy as a fashion-able food-and-wine destination among grape nuts and foodies. Fruit-bombastic Barossa Valley Shiraz and grapefruity New Zealand Sauvignon Blanc from Marlborough have become two of the world's great wine types, even as other regions in both countries produce increasingly noteworthy juice. And South Africa, a country that has been under vine since the seventeenth century, seems to be well on its way to becoming the new Australia. My friend Anthony Hamilton Russell is making incredible Burgundian Pinot Noirs and Chardonnays at the southernmost tip of Africa, in vineyards from which he regularly excavates half-million-year-old hand axes and other artifacts of our earliest ancestors.

In all of these places, advances in viticulture have inevitably been accompanied by the evolution of gastronomy. And in fact my own wine education has brought me gradually into a greater appreciation of food, as has my association with Lora Zarubin, the food editor of *House & Garden,* who almost inevitably accompanies me on these trips. Lora was, for all too brief a period, the owner and chef of Lora's, one of my favorite New York restaurants of the eighties. At the time downtown restaurants were divided into those places where you went to see and be seen and those you went to for the food. Lora's had a surfeit of celebrity patrons, but the food was the real draw; it was a homey place with a refreshingly simple menu at a time when chefs were competing to see how many diverse and incompatible ingredients they could cram into one dish, when every meal seemed to be topped with something along the lines of raspberry chili cilantro vinaigrette with green-tea anchovy sorbet. Ah, yes, the eighties. Who can remember them? Strangely enough, I do remember a sublime grilled chicken I had upstairs at Lora's. When I first saw the menu I didn't know what to make of it—so devoid of frills and flourishes. Where the hell was the chipotle mango pesto? When I later learned she was from San Francisco and a friend of Alice (Chez Panisse) Waters's, her endeavor started to make a lot more sense.

Lora was later recruited by Dominque Browning for *House & Garden,* and it was she who suggested that the magazine should have a wine column, although she was initially highly skeptical when Dominique proposed my name. Ten years later we've spent hundreds of pleasurable hours together—and a few unpleasant ones when we were lost and exhausted and sick of each other on some back road in Provence or Piedmont. (We once spent the better part of a night in a French police station, but that's another story.) Lora's passionate belief that food and wine are inseparable companions has resulted in our working and traveling together. (I suspect she has also convinced upper management at *House & Garden* that I am far too scatterbrained to travel by myself, which is at least half true.) She's organized where I'm improvisational; she is the superego to my id. She drives because my driving makes her nervous. Much of what follows is the result of our travels, racing from winery to trattoria, pilgrims of the palate, devout hedonists in search of the next ecstatic revelation.

It's my ambition to share some of those epiphanies in this book and to encourage readers to seek out their own.

Let's be honest: there's only one activity more satisfying than drinking good wine with good food; and if you're drinking wine in the right company, the one pleasure, more often than not, will lead to the other.

Part One

FOREPLAY

I hate when I'm asked to pick a favorite anything: a book, movie, or song. Sure, I love "Norwegian Wood," but do I like it more than "Angie" or "Alison"? How am I supposed to choose between Kurosawa's *Seven Samurai* and Fellini's *8½*? But I think I can actually say with some certainty that Condrieu is my favorite white wine. I really shouldn't be telling you this, because there's not very much of it made and there never will be: the steep hillsides above the Rhône River on which it's grown are extremely hard to work and the appellation is tiny and nowhere else in the world, not even on similar slopes half a mile north or south of Condrieu, does the Viognier grape produce such sublime juice. Viognier has shown some promise in certain sites in California and elsewhere, but drinking these non-Condrieus is kind of like watching *The Magnificent Seven;* fun, perhaps, but it makes you long for the original.

Why do I like it so much? you may ask. Parsing out the pleasures of Condrieu is a little bit like trying to explicate a haiku. But I can tell you that I love it because white peaches are my favorite fruit and Condrieu frequently tastes like white peaches, though it sometimes verges on apricot. I like its texture, which is fleshy, viscous, and round in the mouth. I like the floral bouquet, which often reminds me of honeysuckle. Certain English tasters equate the aroma with May blossoms, but for me, nonhorticulturalist that I am, it simply reminds me of certain gardens in springtime. I like it because it evokes Gauguin's Tahitian paintings. And finally, perversely, I like it because it lacks two qualities that great wines are supposed to possess; namely, acid and the ability to improve with age. High-acid Riesling is much food-friendlier, and white Burgundy from Meursault or Puligny will last much longer and gain complexity over time. But so what? Love isn't based on practical considerations. Condrieu is a wine for romantics.

Like Côte-Rôtie, the red wine appellation that borders it on the north, Condrieu was nearly moribund after the Second World War, its steep vineyards largely abandoned and its exotic wine on the verge on extinction, until Georges Vernay took over his family domain in the early fifties and became chairman of the appellation, encouraging other landowners to replant the old vineyards even as he lobbied to tighten regulations. Less than twenty acres of Viognier remained on the hills of Condrieu at the time. In 1988 the boundaries of the appellation were limited to the steep hillsides. By the time Vernay's daughter Christine took over the domain in 1997, Condrieu was back in business, the object of a devoted cult of discriminating hedonists.

Based in nearby Ampuis, the Guigal family also deserves credit for resurrecting the great wine of Condrieu. While best known for its Côte-Rôties, the domain founded by Étienne Guigal in 1946 and raised to eminence by son Marcel, who appears to have been born with a beret on his head and a glass wine thief in his hand, is now the largest producer of Condrieu. (Marcel's son Philippe is now working full-time at the domain.) It was a bottle of Guigal Condrieu accompanying a smoked haddock, at the home of novelist Julian Barnes, that initiated my love affair some twenty years ago. In addition to the regular bottling, Guigal produces a luxury cuvée, La Doriane, a rich, decadent bottle of wine that's perfect with foie gras. Certain labels for me are strangely mimetic and inextricably bound up with my sense memories of the wine: Guigal's exotic and wildly floral La Doriane is to my mind perfectly conjured forth by the label, with its intricately detailed and colorful faux–Art Nouveau floral design based on a painting by the Italian painter Moretti.

Another contender for most luxurious Condrieu is André Perret's Coteau de Chéry, from a single vineyard on the Condrieu hillside. The modest and affable Perret has only been making wine since 1983, but the vines for this top cuvée are more than sixty years old. Perret's neighbor Yves Cuilleron produces four separate Condrieux, which ascend the scale from delicate to decadent. His La Petite Côte is a lighter wine that gets an old-fashioned upbringing in tanks and old barrels, while his full-throttle Vertige, which he suggests is perfect for fish in heavier cream sauces (it's also great with many Cantonese dishes) gets the full new-oak treatment. Cuilleron also makes a late-picked Condrieu called Les Ayguets, all honey and hazelnuts, which is essentially a dessert wine, though personally I prefer it on its own or alongside stronger cheeses.

Last May, after a morning tasting in his new winery, the forty-something Cuilleron took me to see one of the vineyards, Les Chaillets, a steep southeast-facing slope looking down over the steely Rhône that was spangled with bright orange poppies. A series of ancient stone terraces seemed to be precariously holding the sandy, granitic soil of the hillside in place. At ten-thirty the sun was just beginning to cut through the morning chill. "They say the Romans built these terraces," Cuilleron said. Perhaps, I said, but I doubt the Romans ever tasted anything quite as honeyed and peachlike and delicate as Cuilleron's '04 Les Chaillets, the memory of which was still vivid an hour after I'd tasted it. It's possible they might not have really appreciated it, Condrieu being decidedly a wine for lovers rather than for fighters.

FRIULI'S FAVORITE SON

Tocai Friulano

Hidden away in the northeastern corner of Italy between the
Alps and the Adriatic, bordered by Austria and Slovenia,
Friuli is an anomaly. Part of the Austro-Hungarian Empire
until 1918, it has a culture and cuisine that seem more Slavic
than Latin. Local pasta tends toward dumplinghood; butter
and lard are at least as common as olive oil. Friuli's prosperity
is based in part on the manufacture of chairs and, increasingly, wine. So far there's no monument to the latter, but you
can see the world's largest chair on the road between Cor-
mons and Udine—an unnerving and surreal sight if you first
encounter it at one in the morning after a festive night at La
Frasca, the taverna owned by winemaker Valter Scarbolo and
his wife. Although some interesting reds are made here, Friuli
is best known to wine lovers as the source of Italy's finest white
wines, the most distinctive of which is Tocai Friulano.

Friulian wines, unlike most of the wines of Europe, are
usually named for their grape varietals. Because of its complicated history and vine-friendly climate, Friuli is home to
many French and German varietals, such as Riesling, Sauvignon Blanc, and Chardonnay, as well as to local grapes
like Ribolla, Picolit, and Malvasia. Most Friulian wineries
turn out varietals as well as blended "super-whites." With the

exception of the Loire Valley, Friuli may be the best place in Europe for Sauvignon Blanc; but for most wineries, Tocai is the benchmark—the hometown favorite. The locals often start the day with a glass of Tocai, calling out in the local dialect for a *tai di vin*—but it's not just for breakfast anymore.

The history of Tocai is obscure, and its name seems to come from the Hungarian region that produces dessert wines from the Furmint grape, but the Friulians consider Tocai their signature local grape, an indispensable accompaniment to the salami and prosciutto that start every meal here. Indeed, prosciutto and Tocai seem to be one of those magical marriages made in the soil, like Sancerre and chèvre, or Chablis and oysters. Sipping a Zamo Tocai at the tiny Enoteca Lavaroni in the village of Manzano, with a platter of Lorenzo d'Osvaldo artisanal prosciutto, I experienced one of those moments of sensual satori that gourmands live for. The Friulians insist on the superiority of the local Prosciutto San Daniele over Prosciutto di Parma, but Tocai works very nicely with both, as it does with speck, Spanish ham, Virginia ham, and most things fatty, smoky, and salty. And that's just for starters. Appropriately, for a grape born so close to the Adriatic, Tocai is also a dream date for seafood.

"Tocai is crisp, but it also has weight on the palate," says Morgan Rich, the wine director at Del Posto in New York, which generally features a dozen or so Tocais from Friuli on its list. Tocai's pearlike fruit is balanced by a refreshing lemony acidity and mineral highlights. It can resemble a blend of Riesling and Sauvignon Blanc. Friuli made its reputation with bright, refreshing, stainless-steel-fermented whites, and most winemakers think Tocai is best kept away from wood, although Borgo San Daniele and Miani both make compelling barrel-aged examples.

"Tocai is absolutely one of the great food wines," claims Joseph Bastianich, a first-generation American whose family hails from Friuli. "It's versatile and flexible—you can make young, fruity, early-drinking wine or a bigger wine that ages." The burly baron of a food-and-wine empire that encompasses some of New York's most acclaimed Italian restaurants, including Babbo and Felidia, Bastianich has an eponymous wine estate in the hills of the Colli Orientali region of Friuli, where he makes an old-vine Tocai that he turbocharges with a healthy dose of late-harvest, botrytis-infected grapes. Bastianich's Tocai Plus, grown on steep hillsides in the town of Buttrio, is a prime example of the fatter style of Tocai—a Botero of a wine—which can stand up to dishes like *stinco di vitello* (roasted veal shank) and which Bastianich likes to drink with full-flavored cheeses. His young winemaker, Emilio Del Medico, makes a similarly rich and powerful Tocai called Tocai Vigne Cinquant'Anni, at the nearby property Zamo, as well as the more typical, lighter-style Tocai Friulano. The Zamo family made their fortune manufacturing chairs, and they seem to have spent a fair chunk of it on a new, computerized, underground winery just down the hill from the thirteenth-century Abbey of Rosazzo.

The most complex Tocais come from the hillside vineyards of Collio and Colli Orientali, a kind of meteorological intersection of the cool Alpine climate and the warm Adriatic. The other prime area is the Isonzo Valley, which is naturally air-conditioned by an Alpine breeze called the bora that funnels through a gap in the foothills. Some other names to seek out: Ronco del Gelso, Villa Russiz, Edi Keber, Polencic, Scubla, and Marco Felluga.

The best way to get acquainted with Tocai is to sit down with a bottle alongside a plate of salami or prosciutto. But almost any grilled fish would be happy to make the acquaintance of this versatile grape.

THIN IS IN

The New Wave of California Chardonnays

My very first wine column was about California Chardonnay, a genre about which I was somewhat skeptical. In the mid-1990s, the typical premium Napa or Sonoma Chardonnay had much in common with a vanilla milk shake or, figuratively speaking, with the then reigning queen of *Baywatch,* Pamela Anderson. Such superpremium winemakers as Marcassin, Kistler, Peter Michael, and Talbott transcended the genre—creating a new standard of richness, power, and concentration through the application of Burgundian methods to superripe California grapes—with uniquely opulent results. Too many of their neighbors, however, were making whites that were merely fat, loud, and sunburned.

It may be a coincidence that I started noticing a new generation of Chardonnays at about the same time that Pamela Anderson announced her plans for a breast reduction. (I know, Pam reaugmented. I can live with that.) But in tastings and in talking with some of the makers of newly minted Chardonnay labels, I am finding a refreshing emphasis on finesse and subtlety. The wine world, like any other, has its trends and fashions, and in the realm of high-end Cal Chard, thin is in. Words like *elegant* and *racy* and *lean* are now being held up as ideals. Even *nervous* is good. It means—I think—

acidic, and *acidity* is no longer a bad word. (Acid is essentially the skeleton on which the sugary flesh of the grape is draped.)

California Chardonnay makers have always talked about Burgundy as a model; it is, after all, the homeland of Chardonnay, and of such great Chardonnay wines as Montrachet and Meursault. But even the cooler areas of California, like Carneros, the Russian River Valley, and the Santa Ynez Valley, are warmer than Burgundy—and of course the soils are different. Applying the same techniques will yield different results. Seldom does California achieve the crisp sculptural definition or the mineral notes of white Burgundy; nor does Burgundy often achieve the tropical-fruit decadence of California Chard. "You can't make Montrachet in much of California—it's just too warm," says David Ramey, who started making Chardonnay under his own name in 1996. "But you can still aim for a balance between richness and finesse."

Ramey's recent Chardonnays exemplify the new, crisp, elegant style, although he likes to call it "retro," since his methods are traditional and minimalist. With his wire-rim specs and salt-and-pepper hair, Ramey is pretty elegant and crisp himself, dressing with a certain minimalist, expensively casual flair, which is unusual in Napa wine cellars. He developed his winemaking chops at Chalk Hill, Simi, Matanzas Creek, and Dominus. Until recently he was a consultant at Rudd, which he propelled into the spotlight, but he parted to concentrate on the Ramey label. Although Ramey's Chards have plenty of ripe fruit, they also have a vibrant wire of acidity, which distinguishes them from many California Chards. Tasted against a Kistler Durell Vineyard, Ramey's Hyde Vineyard Chardonnay seems like a Modigliani displayed beside a Botero.

Another rising Chardonnay star is Robert Sinskey, who first made his name with Pinot and Merlot. The wine from his biodynamically farmed Three Amigos Vineyard in Carneros has a Puligny-Montrachet-like steeliness, sort of like a Ginsu blade concealed in a pineapple. Sinskey gets his zingy acidity in part by skipping malolactic, the secondary fermentation that softens the malic acid. "In California," he says, "our challenge is maintaining acidity. It doesn't make sense to soften the acid only to add it back artificially"—which is what many California makers do (the addition of tartaric acid being SOP in California). Sinskey's style is more food-friendly—almost the raison d'être for acid in a wine. "You don't want a milk shake with your fish," Sinskey says. "It used to be about competition, about creating blockbusters. Now it's about consumption and cuisine." Sinskey attributes the new subtlety of many California Chards in part to a new appreciation for the vineyard itself, and a de-emphasis on high-tech interventionist techniques.

Ted Lemon at Littorai is as qualified as anyone to toss the word *Burgundian* around, having been the winemaker for Domaine Guy Roulot in Meursault from 1982 to 1984. In cool Meursault he tried to pick as late as possible, but in Littorai's western Sonoma vineyards he picks earlier than many of his neighbors, in order to keep the wines from getting too flabby. Like Sinskey, Lemon tries to avoid the blockbuster style—the big, fat, oaky, buttery fruit bomb. However impressive, these buxom Chardonnays overwhelm everything but lobster with butter. "There's a disconnect," Lemon says, "between the elegance and finesse in our cuisine and in our wine."

Down in the cool valleys north of Santa Barbara, a leaner, edgier style of Chardonnay has been more common than in Napa and Sonoma. Relative newcomers Greg Brewer and Steve Clifton, under the Brewer-Clifton label, are making some of the most radically nervous New World Chardonnays ever—so crisp and vibrant that I have mistaken them for Chablis. Hirsute, voluble Jim Clendenen, whose personal style is heavy metal/Hell's Angel, makes some of the most subtle and ageworthy Chardonnays in the New World. Once literally a voice in the wilderness—in the Santa Maria Valley—he has been making svelte Burgundian Chardonnays for two decades, and has influenced many of those who have followed him to this region. "The most important thing is to pick grapes in balance," says Clendenen, who scoffs at the notion that a Chardonnay with 15 percent alcohol could possibly have balance, and who has often been criticized for picking underripe grapes. Clendenen, who has been in and out of fashion several times since his start in 1982, believes that the American wine world is definitely coming back in his direction.

THE WHITES OF THE ANDES

Los Andes, the snowcapped, skyscraping mountain range that separates Chile from Argentina, is one of the few things the two countries have in common. Chile is sometimes called the Switzerland of South America; Argentina is a lot like Italy, only more so. International bankers love Chile; Argentina not so long ago welshed on some $151 billion in loans. Chileans generally respect traffic signs and speed limits, while Argentines drive the way bats fly, hell-bent, obeying their own personal radar. But thanks to the Andes, the countries have something else in common: the lower slopes and plateaus on both sides are a viticultural paradise. The French, not exactly famous for respecting terroir other than their own, have been paying close attention to this bounty, and at this point you can hardly pop a Champagne cork in a hotel lobby on either side of the Andes without hitting a winemaker or château owner from Bordeaux.

While the red wines of the two countries are distinct enough to merit separate treatment, the whites produced from French varietals on both slopes are fairly similar in quality and style, and more than ready to compete in world markets. Viognier, Pinot Gris, and Chenin Blanc may make the cut someday, but Sauvignon Blanc and especially Chardonnay are the smart buys for now.

The Argentine landscape is characterized by sweeping, big-sky American vistas, whereas on the Chilean side the vineyards of the Central Valley are bounded on one side by the coastal range and on the other by the Andes, frequently shrouded in mist. The vines arrived with the missionaries who followed the conquistadors and flourished in idyllic isolation, miraculously escaping the worldwide phylloxera blight of the nineteenth century. This viticultural Eden was home to a half dozen huge domestic wineries, like Cousiño Macul and Concha y Toro, which prospered by quenching the local thirst for heavy reds. But it was the founding of Montes by a quartet of Chilean wine-industry veterans, including Aurelio Montes, in 1988 that signaled the beginning of the modern, export-oriented era. In the early '90s, as Augusto Pinochet's long dictatorship gave way to a democratically elected government, Chile began to attract foreign wine capital.

The ocean-cooled Casablanca region, north of Santiago, has proven ideal for Chardonnay—Montes sources its Chardonnay grapes from the area, as does the venerable firm Errázuriz. Today, Casablanca is the source of the best Chilean Chards, many the product of French and American investment. Chilean-born Agustín F. Huneeus, who became a major figure in Napa as president of Franciscan, cofounded the Veramonte estate in Casablanca in 1990. Almost simultaneously, Alexandra Marnier-Lapostolle, granddaughter of the creator of Grand Marnier, founded Casa Lapostolle and hired Michel Rolland, the world's most famous flying oenologist, as consulting winemaker. They chose Casablanca for the Chardonnay vineyards, planting on a series of steep hillsides. Chilean viticulture has been largely a valley-floor affair, but Lapostolle's example is being followed by others. This past April, on the verge of the harvest, I spent a morning tromping those hilly vineyards with the wry, multilingual Rolland. Long after his neighbors on the flats had harvested, he plucked and tasted grapes, deciding which parcels to pick first. This hillside farming is expensive, requiring drip irrigation, but the results speak for themselves.

Jacques and François Lurton, scions of the great Bordeaux family, have wineries on both sides of the Andes. Their Gran Araucano Sauvignon Blanc is probably Chile's best—no surprise, since their family produces some of the finest white Bordeaux. Fortunately for the brothers, the plane trip between Santiago, Chile, and Mendoza, Argentina, is just about an hour.

The low-rise, canal-laced city of Mendoza is the center of fine-wine production in Argentina. The canal system, which dates back to the original Indian inhabitants, extends throughout Mendoza Province, bringing runoff from the Andes to the orchards and vineyards of the arid region. The "terraces," or plateaus, that rise toward the eastern slopes of the Andes in a series of climactic gradations provide successively cooler microclimates that can essentially be matched to the ripening requirements of different grapes. Vines have flourished here since the late 1500s, but the dawn of modern viticulture might be dated from the arrival of the French firm Moët & Chandon, which established a huge sparkling-wine facility in 1960. In the mid-1990s, Chandon founded a still-wine domaine, Terrazas de Los Andes, refurbishing an 1898 winery and planting new vineyards. Its Chardonnay vineyards occupy the highest terraces, above three thousand feet.

Catena Zapata, with its new Jetsons-meets-the-Mayans winery, traces its roots back to 1899, although its modern era begins in 1982, when third-generation Nicolás Catena had an epiphany while visiting the Robert Mondavi winery in Napa and decided to take the family's plonk factory upmarket. The three Chardonnays produced here, starting with the ten-dollar Alamos bottlings, represent exceptional value. Bodega Norton, founded in 1895 by an Englishman to satisfy the Argentine thirst for cheap, oxidized reds, has undergone a similar transformation and now produces the best Sauvignon Blanc that I encountered in Argentina.

At prices ranging from ten to twenty-five dollars, Chilean and Argentine Chardonnays represent a great value these days, in part because of low land and labor costs. They also seem to have more natural acidity than other New World examples, which makes for more refreshing summer drinking. You don't have to picture the snowcapped Andes in the background as you sip them in the dog days, but I know I will.

The white wines of Graves have an image problem. Bordeaux is practically synonymous with red wine, which accounts for about 85 percent of its vast production. Made from Sauvignon Blanc and Sémillon, white Bordeaux remains something of an enigma to the average American consumer—less glamorous than the reds or the Chardonnay-based whites of Burgundy.

Situated to the south of the city of Bordeaux, the Graves appellation is the home of most of the best Bordeaux whites. Connoisseurs have long sought out the ageworthy whites from Haut-Brion, Laville-Haut-Brion and Domaine de Chevalier. I've been collecting them just long enough to start appreciating their amazing potential. At a recent dinner party I hosted, the '83 Laville, which was like liquified crème brûlée and peaches, aroused far more favorable comment among the grape nuts than the mature (and expensive) Burgundies that followed.

The best vineyards of the Graves district are set in the midst of the congested suburbs of Talence and Pessac. The vineyards of Haut-Brion, with its sixteenth-century château, occupy a gravelly hillock amidst a rising tide of boxy housing complexes. Best known for its first-growth red wine, Haut-Brion also makes small quantities of ethereal white. Across the treacherously busy street are the vineyards of La Mission–Haut-Brion (red) and Laville-Haut-Brion (white), which in 1983 were purchased by Haut-Brion's owners, the Dillon family. Winemaking on both sides of the street is overseen by one of the great statesmen of Bordeaux, Jean Delmas, who was born at Haut-Brion.

Like the reds—for that matter, like most siblings—Haut-Brion blanc and Laville-Haut-Brion have separate and distinctive personalities, despite their physical proximity and a shared winemaking team—a good argument for the importance of terroir. Laville has a higher percentage of Sémillon, which is fleshier and oilier than the snappy, high-strung, citric Sauvignon Blanc; in partnership, these two grapes help give white Bordeaux its unique, balanced, food-friendly character.

Drive down the road, turn right at the *rocade,* or ring road, and if you watch very carefully you'll eventually see the sign for Domaine de Chevalier—a sea of vines surrounded by dense pine forest. The single-story château is modest and homey by Bordeaux standards, although proprietor Olivier Bernard and his wife, Anne, must be one of the best-looking couples in the region. Their domain has the benefit of deep gravelly soil and the misfortune to be among the most frost- and hail-ridden patches of all Bordeaux. In those years when neither affliction strikes, Domaine de Chevalier produces, in addition to its red, a complex and haunting white, which improves and develops in bottle for years. As in nearby Sauternes, the grapes here are picked in several *passages* to guarantee optimal ripeness.

The Big Three whites of Graves, all located in the recently

created Pessac-Léognan appellation, are relatively expensive and hard to find; but for about half the price of a village Mersault you can find some smokin', early-drinking white Graves, thanks in no small measure to the work of white-wine-making guru and consulting oenologist Denis Dubourdieu. Dubourdieu invented a technique—rare for whites—that leaves the skins in contact with the juice. Besides his own properties, Clos Floridene and Reynon, Dubourdieu consults for many of the best white-wine producers, including Domaine de Chevalier. He was responsible for making de Fieuzal a collector's favorite, beginning with the '85 vintage, and for improving the supple and fragrant whites of the ancient domain of Carbonnieux, the largest producer of white Graves. Dubourdieu's son Jean-Philippe produces another fine white at Château d'Archambeau.

Smith-Haut-Lafitte, one of Graves' many underperformers over the years, has cleaned up its act since changing hands in 1990. Its white wine represents an extreme of the modern trend toward bright, sassy Sauvignons fermented in new oak, which are aimed at the international palate. Tasty as it is, I think the genius of the region is better reflected in a blend with a larger proportion of Sémillon and a lesser proportion of new oak—à la Dubourdieu. But this new style is certainly preferable to the oversulfured, fruit-deficient wines that were the norm fifteen years ago. It's worth mentioning that the Cathiard family opened a luxurious modern spa on the property in 1999—a godsend for a region seriously underendowed with good hotels. Although, having not yet visited, I can't begin to guess what "vinotherapy" might be. Bathing in wine?

Some stars and rising stars: Chantegrive, Coubins-Lurton, La Louvière, Malartic-Lagravière, Pape-Clément, and La Tour Martillac. Outside of the Graves appellation there are a few whites worth seeking out, including those of the famed Châteaux Margaux and Lynch-Bages. Although not a great red-wine vintage, 2004 was a significantly better year for white Graves, and the 2005s should be at least as good. Either of these vintages will drink well over the next few years in conjunction with white fish, grilled chicken, or sheep's milk and goat's milk cheese. The Big Three usually taste delicious in youth and then go into hibernation for several years. If you should be lucky enough to find an older vintage, like an '89 Chevalier or a '94 Haut-Brion, treat it with all due respect—get some turbot or Dover sole and share it with someone whose gratitude you'd like to cultivate.

NO RESPECT

Soave

The view from the exit ramp of the autostrada is emblematic of the problem with Soave. The first thing you see through your windshield is a huge lime-green warehouse with a batwing roofline that looks like some kind of retro-futuristic vision from the animators of the Powerpuff Girls. Off in the hazy distance, floating dreamlike above the big SOAVE BOLLA sign atop the warehouse, you can see the medieval ramparts of Soave castle perched on a distant hilltop. From the ridiculous to the sublime . . .

They ought to post a CAVEAT EMPTOR sign beside the exit.

Soave is the "the most maligned, misunderstood and polarized wine district in Italy," according to Italophiles Joe Bastianich and David Lynch, authors of the indispensible *Vino Italiano.* Most of us think of Soave as the insipid white beverage of our ignorant youth. But there are a handful of stubborn idealists who produce exceptional wines from the native Garganega grapes in the rolling hills just east of Verona.

It says a lot about the current situation in Soave that one of the two finest producers has recently divorced himself from the appellation, removing the Soave name from his labels. "It's water," he says of the average Soave. "No aroma, no taste." Roberto Anselmi is a Porsche-driving, black–Prada-clad native of the region whose genial and gregarious nature keeps rubbing up against his fierce perfectionism. Shortly after he welcomes me into his sleek modernist suite of offices in the village of Monteforte, he throws a small tantrum about the faint ammoniac residue of some cleaning products in the tasting room and instructs his daughter to move our tasting to the nearby winery, while making a note to chastise the cleaning staff. In many ways he reminds me of Angelo Gaja, another hypomanic Italian who inherited a wine estate in a backwater appellation and decided to conquer the world.

Anselmi's father was a successful negotiant who turned out millions of bottles of undistinguished plonk from purchased grapes. After returning to the family seat with an oenology degree and high moral purpose, Roberto closed down the negotiant business and set about, in concert with his friend and neighbor Leonildo Pieropan, "to make a revolution."

The revolution started, as is so often the case, in the hills. Or maybe it was a counterrevolution: the traditional Soave Classico district encompassed only the hillsides, with their poor volcanic and calcareous soils. In 1968, when the official Soave DOC was created by the Italian authorities, pressure from the big growers resulted in a huge expansion of the zone to include vast swatches of fertile, overproductive flatland. (Ignoring the ancient Roman maxim: Bacchus loves the hills.) Anselmi concentrated his efforts on the steep hillsides and adapted new viticultural practices to replace the old superproductive pergola system. Beginning in the late seventies he started producing serious, rich Soaves and lobbied fiercely for stricter regulations.

Anselmi failed to convince the authorities to hold his neighbors to a higher standard. "After twenty-five years I decided to divorce Soave," he says. So you will just have to take my word for it that Anselmi's wines are essentially Soaves—the essence of what garganega (accented with a little aromatic Trebbiano di Soave) from this region can produce—a wine with more body and fruit than the average Italian white and mineral highlights that can make it reminiscent of a good Chablis.

Anselmi's friend Leonildo Pieropan remains married to the Soave appellation; he and his forebears are undoubtedly the best thing that ever happened to this slatternly tramp of a wine region. Stylistically and temperamentally he is the opposite of his friend Anselmi: a shy, bespectacled homebody who favors cardigans and lives with his family in a meticulously restored villa just inside the crenelated medieval walls of the town of Soave.

Despite his reputation as the ultimate traditionalist, Pieropan loves technology, and the medieval outbuildings around the house are crammed with the latest in computer-controlled, stainless-steel fermentation tanks. His vineyards, like Anselmi's, are located exclusively in the hills of the Classico region, and his wines have long been cherished by connoisseurs around the world for their purity, delicacy, and balance. His single-vineyard La Rocca is one of Italy's greatest white wines. Unlike most Soaves, Pieropan's wines have the ability to age for ten years and beyond, becoming increasingly minerally over time. They are the best possible proof that the region is worth saving.

———

A few other producers are making noteworthy wines, including brothers Graziano and Sergio Pra, whose single-vineyard Monte Grande Soave, made from grapes with a serious case of vertigo, is consistently one of the best wines of the region. The Gini brothers, Sandro and Claudio, make a rich, plump style of Soave, as does Stefano Inama. Inama's regular Soave is very good, but he has made a name for himself in a hurry with two supercharged, wood-aged, single-vineyard wines, Foscarino and Vigneto du Lot, which are deemed freakish by some traditionalists, tasting somewhat like superripe New World Chardonnays. Whether you like this style or not, they are an excellent antidote to the notion that Soave is a dilute and boring quaff.

A few other names to look for: Cantina del Castello, Coffele, and Suavia. There may be a few good makers I'm unaware of, but the six and a half million bottles a year from other sources are probably worth avoiding. Soave's reputation as a reservoir of cheap mouthwash works in favor of the consumer; the regular bottlings of the top producers sell for ten to fifteen bucks and the single vineyard wines are in the twenty-dollar range. They are perfect summer whites—especially in this market.

GRAY IS THE NEW WHITE

Pinot Gris

Back in the 1980s, I remember seeing a graffito in Milan that read NO MORE GRAY. The slogan was a young fashionista's battle cry against the muted palette of Armani and his followers, but it might also have applied to the Pinot Grigio (gray Pinot) that was coming out of Italy at the time, which was at least as dull as a gray suit. When I first tasted a great Pinot Gris from Alsace, I didn't even make the connection between this ambrosia and the stuff we used to swill by the bucket at Elaine's. Pinot Gris, Tokay (as it is sometimes called in Alsace), and Pinot Grigio are from one and the same grape—although the northern and southern styles vary considerably. Some brilliant PGs have begun to emerge from Friuli, in northern Italy. And, in recent years, the grape has also found a new home in Oregon's Willamette Valley, alongside Pinot Noir.

Pinot Gris, a.k.a. Pinot Grigio, is, in fact, a mutation of Pinot Noir that probably first appeared in the vineyards of Burgundy. It is so named because the grapes, when ripe, can often appear gray-blue (as well as brownish pink). In rare instances, a producer may leave the juice on the skins long enough for it to pick up some color; but, generally speaking, Pinot Gris makes a food-friendly white wine. Pinot Gris reaches its apogee in Alsace, where it yields rich, full-bodied, profound wines—some in a sweeter, dessert style—that can age for decades. The average Pinot Grigio is made in a crisper, lighter style. Oregon, where the French name is used, seems to be staking out some middle ground.

Pinot Gris was introduced in Oregon by the same man who first planted Pinot Noir there back in 1965: former philosophy major, dental student, and University of California at Davis oenology graduate David Lett of Eyrie Vineyards. (Lett's Pinot Gris, like his Pinot Noir, seems to be built for aging, and can be ungenerous in its youth.) Today there are more than a thousand acres planted in the Willamette Valley, and Pinot Gris has surpassed Chardonnay as the signature white grape of the region. The Alsatians don't seem to be trembling in their boots just yet, and the hype is well ahead of the overall quality, but Oregon Pinot Gris has become popular enough to inspire vintners in California and Washington State to plant the varietal.

At its best, Oregon Pinot Gris tastes a little like ripe pears, with spicy, smoky highlights, and it complements a wide variety of foods, especially when the winemakers lay off the new oak barrels. The food match of choice in the Pacific Northwest is grilled salmon, but Pinot Gris also suits—far better than the average Chardonnay—Dungeness crab, oysters, and even grilled pork and sausages. "It has a unique spicy quality that goes well with Asian and fusion cuisine," says Mark Vlossak of St. Innocent Winery, in Salem, Oregon. "It works really well with fish and game birds and even vegetarian cuisines. Pinot Gris also transmits the signature of the land better than Chardonnay." Generally, it is made in a dry style, in keeping with American tastes, although one or two late-harvest sweet-style wines from the 1999 vintage were available recently, notably at St. Innocent, where Vlossak, a genial and intense native of Wisconsin, is producing Oregon's finest Pinot Gris.

Vlossak's love of the grape was inspired back in 1991 by an encounter with a bottle of Livio Felluga's benchmark Pinot Grigio from Friuli. "We had it with gravlax, and it blew everything else on the table away," he says. "I spent two years searching for the right vineyard. In '93, I made the first Pinot Gris. I started making it from this vineyard in a northern Italian style. My distributor in Seattle said to me, 'You should go to Alsace. You don't know shit about Pinot Gris in Oregon.' " Vlossak's trip to Alsace, and his meeting with the charismatic André Ostertag—who has since become a friend—expanded Vlossak's perception of the potential for Pinot Gris. "I decided it's possible to make the dry, *grand cru* style of Pinot Gris here," he says. The problem is that Oregon Pinot Gris is perceived by both winemakers and the public to be an inexpensive Chardonnay alternative. In order to make great Pinot Gris, good sites need to be chosen and yields have to be slashed, which represents a sacrifice. The catch-22 is that growers and winemakers need an economic incentive to raise quality, but until quality improves, it's tough to sell a bottle of Pinot Gris for more than fifteen bucks, while Oregon Pinot Noir can sell for fifty or sixty dollars a bottle. St. Innocent's recent Shea Vineyard bottlings—from a site also famous for Pinot Noir—could help change perceptions of the future of this grape in Oregon.

Fortunately, a handful of Oregon wineries—including

Belle Pente, Evesham Wood, and Lemelson—are also making very good Pinot Gris. Oregon winemakers haven't yet agreed to standardize the bottle shape for this varietal. Some use the slope-shouldered Burgundy bottle, while others favor the long, tall, Alsatian bottle. My unscientific conclusion, after tasting twenty bottles of the 2000 vintage, is that the best makers favor the Alsatian bottle, bravely flying in the face of its negative association—at least in the minds of many American wine drinkers—with cheap German wine. Remember Blue Nun? Forget it. Try a Pinot Gris the next time you grill a fish.

Hugh Johnson once remarked that he was surprised that no university had endowed a chair in German wine labeling. For most English speakers, such is the perceived complexity of the Gothic-looking labels, with their information overload and their terrifying terminology, that they make Burgundy seem simple by comparison. Trockenbeerenauslese Graacher Himmelreich, anyone? Even hardened wine wonks ask themselves whether life is long enough to learn the difference between *Spätlese* and *Auslese*. (Admit it—you're scared already.) German winemakers have long recognized this dilemma without necessarily knowing what the hell to do about it. Lately, though, some of Germany's best Riesling producers are wooing American consumers with simplified labels.

One technical term that's worth mastering is *Kabinett,* the lightest of five "predicates" indicating levels of ripeness. For midsummer drinking, a low alcohol, off-dry *Kabinett* from the Mosel region is, to my mind, one of the few beverages that can compete with a nice dry pilsner. And Riesling *Kabinetts* are quite possibly the most versatile food wines in the world— perfect not only for lighter fish, chicken, and pork preparations but also for sweet and spicy Asian, Mexican, and fusion dishes.

Those of you who won't be able to remember the term *Kabinett* five minutes after you finish this column are not necessarily out of luck. Raimund Prüm, of S. A. Prüm in the Mosel, understands your anxiety about German labels. Prum owns vines in some of the greatest vineyards in Germany, perched on steep, sun-trapping slopes high above the Mosel River, including Wehlener Sonnenuhr, named after the now famous sundial that his great-great-grandfather Jodicus Prüm constructed in the vineyard in 1848. And one of these days, after you've developed an appreciation for great Riesling, you may remember the name of this vineyard, planted on blue slate, which is believed to impart a distinctive stony flavor to the wines. In the meantime, you can probably remember the term *Blue Slate,* which is the name of the off-dry *Kabinett*-level Riesling that had its debut in this country with the '03 vintage, and risk the fifteen bucks to give it a try. Prüm also makes a lighter, slightly sweeter, nicely fruity ten-dollar bottle called Essence, which is my new Chinese-takeout default beverage setting.

Prüm's roots in the region go deep; he says his family has been in the Mosel for 850 years. His roots also go tall—his grandfather Sebastian A., who served in Kaiser Wilhelm's Dragoon Bodyguard, stood six foot nine. Prüm himself tops out at a mere six-four, crowned with unruly flaming red hair, which has earned him the nickname "der Specht"—the woodpecker. I suspect the name also derives from the way he bobs his head as he gets excited talking about his wines, which can be pretty damned thrilling at the higher end. (The wines, not his head bobbing.) Every wine lover should eventually taste a great *Eiswein* (ice wine) like his 1998 from the Graacher Himmelreich vineyard, the frozen grapes of which were picked the morning of December 16.

The affable, puckish Raimund has a slew of relatives in the area who are also making Riesling under various, somewhat confusing Prüm-inflected labels, including the great Joh. Jos. Prüm and Dr. F. Weins-Prüm. (They take their doctorates seriously in Germany, and every other winemaker seems to use the title.) Another great Mosel producer is Dr. Ernst Loosen, *Decanter* magazine's 2005 Man of the Year. Loosen's Wehlener Sonnenuhrs are always brilliant, long-lived wines, but he also bottles a *Kabinett*-level wine made from several vineyards, called Dr. L., which is a good value and a great, not-too-serious summertime quaff. In collaboration with Chateau Ste. Michelle, in Washington State, Loosen also makes a very fine Riesling, Eroica.

Simplified labeling, of course, is hardly a guarantee of quality. It was Blue Nun and Black Tower, after all, that created the stereotype of German whites as the vinous equivalent of Dunkin' Donuts. The most important element on a German wine label is the maker's name, and in order to experience the torquey and transcendent pleasures of Geman Riesling you need to memorize a few. Lingenfelder's Bird Label and Selbach's (of Selbach-Oster) Fish Label are two entry-level Rieslings from serious makers, and both offer good value at about ten bucks.

At a slightly more ambitious level are Dragonstone from Leitz, J. J. Riesling from Christoffel, and "Jean Baptiste" from Gunderloch. Robert Weil's top Rieslings from the Rheinghau are among the most sought after and expensive in Germany, but he bottles a *Kabinett* and a wine called simply Riesling, which, particularly in the last three vintages—'02, '03, and '04—should be approached with caution, lest you find yourself developing a serious Riesling habit. It's a little like reading *A Portrait of the Artist as a Young Man*. Next thing you know, you're neck-deep in *Ulysses* or, God forbid, *Finnegans Wake,* which, come to think of it, is the literary equivalent of *Trockenbeerenauslese.*

Part Two

"ALL WINE WISHES
IT COULD BE RED"

In recent years the archetypal fantasy of starting a small winery has become more and more fantastic; in Napa the start-up
cost for a small vineyard with a winery is now generally reck-
oned at around seven to ten million dollars and the ATF bonds
required to open new wineries are scarcer than magnums
of Screaming Eagle. But down the coast in Santa Barbara
County there are dozens of tiny new bootstrap wineries oper-
ating out of sheds and warehouse spaces in rural industrial
parks, and they seem to be multiplying like Kennedys. While
Pinot Noir has become the established star of the region, these
upstarts are mostly making Syrah, in their aluminum-sided
sheds—in part out of necessity, good Pinot grapes having
become scarce and expensive, and in part out of a conviction
of its great potential in the area, thanks to pioneering Rhône
Rangers like Alban and Qupé.

The typical Santa Barbara shedista narrative goes like this:
you start working in the cellar of a bigger winery and learn
the ropes: the region, the vineyards, and the growers. Eventually you borrow from relatives and max out your credit cards
to rent a shed, buy a few tanks and a few tons of Syrah, design
a label, and make your own wine. You share equipment and
wine notes with friends. And you keep your day job in the
meantime.

A classic example is Kenneth-Crawford, started in '01 by Joey Gummere and Mark Horvath. (The name combines their two middle names.) "Mark and I met working in the cellars of Babcock," Gummere told me recently. "You see how things on a smaller scale can be so much better." Gummere moved on to Lafond, another midsized winery, before teaming up with Horvath in '01 to produce four barrels of Syrah from the Lafond and Melville vineyards, two relatively cool sites in the Santa Rita Hills appellation. As of the '05 vintage they are producing fifteen hundred cases—quite a lot on the shedista scale. When I visited a couple of years ago, Kenneth-Crawford was sharing a 2,400-square-foot shed with Jason Drew, another Babcock alum, who started Drew Family Cellars (sounds better than Drew Family Shed, I guess) in 2001 and who has been producing beautiful red monsters ever since.

Benjamin Silver, of the eponymous Silver Wines, identifies 2001 as a watershed vintage for the new landless winemakers; that's when a number of non–winery affiliated vineyards started producing Syrah in sufficient quantities to sell. "This offered access to Rhône varietals to us smaller guys and gals," Silver says. Some of these vineyards were planted in '95, when the '93 Zaca Mesa Syrah made the No. 6 slot of *Wine Spectator*'s Top 100 list, at the same time that Manfred Krankl's first Sine Qua Non bottlings were drawing attention to the potential for Syrah in the Santa Barbara area. Silver, who worked at Zaca Mesa at the time, has since gone on to create his own label, which includes several Syrahs.

"I used to make Pinot under my own label, and then it got

hard to find," says Santa Barbara native Kris Curran, who turned to Syrah after losing her Pinot sources in the 2000 vintage. Curran made a name for herself as the winemaker for Sea Smoke, the new Santa Rita Hills star. She makes Sea Smoke Pinot and Curran Syrah in an industrial park in Lompoc, which its winemaking denizens refer to as the "ghetto." The ghetto is home to half a dozen small, ambitious Syrah producers, including Steve Clifton of Brewer-Clifton fame, who makes a Syrah under the Alder label, and Chad Melville, who serves as the viticulturalist for his family's eponymous winery by day and makes several Syrahs with his wife, Mary, under the Samsara label. Melville shares his shed in the ghetto with three friends: Sashi Moorman and Peter Hunken, who pay the rent with jobs at Stolpman Vineyards, and Jim Knight, whose family owns Wine House, a Los Angeles wine store. Knight, a former rock-and-roll drummer and cellar rat at Lafond, makes a Syrah under the Jelly Roll label, while Moorman and Hunken's label is Piedrasassi. (Confused yet?) And together they make a wine called Holus Bolus. "We're all good friends," Melville says. "We purchased equipment and formed an LLC. Our press and destemmer alone cost us $130,000. None of us could do it on our own, but collectively we could afford good equipment."

The other HQ for the shedista movement is Central Coast Wine Services, a so-called custom-crush facility in Santa Maria, which provides winery equipment and storage space to many of Santa Barbara County's low-budget oenologists, including Benjamin Silver and Seth Kunin, a transplanted New Yorker who bailed on med school to work at the Wine

Cask in Santa Barbara, the retail headquarters of the local wine revolution. Kunin fermented his first batch of purchased grapes in a garbage can at the store and later got a job in the cellar at the Gainey Vineyard. As a fan of the northern Rhône, he was drawn to Syrah, and now makes several Côte-Rôtie wannabes under his own label while maintaining his day job at Westerly Vineyards.

You get the distinct feeling that this scrappy communal spirit and note sharing must be good for the wine. Some great juice is coming out of these unglamorous sheds, and at an average price of around thirty-five dollars for a single-vineyard, small-production wine they make cult Cabs seem grossly overpriced. Santa Barbara County in the first decade of the twenty-first century is sort of the oenological equivalent of Silicon Valley in the '70s or Paris in the '20s. If you want to get in on a very good thing, get on some of these mailing lists.

I'm supposed to meet two different Côte-Rôtie winemakers on the same day in the same church parking lot in the same tiny village—one at eleven and another at two in the afternoon. Easy enough, except that they are former friends, i.e., mortal enemies. Their American distributor has repeatedly warned me not to mention the name of one to the other— they had a nasty falling-out over the purchase of a vineyard. I guess this is what *The Oxford Companion to Wine* means when it calls Côte-Rôtie "a hotbed of activity and ambition."

As recently as twenty years ago, no one was fighting very hard to buy land on the steep hillsides above the village of Ampuis. Côte-Rôtie, the "roasted slope," was so named because its southeast exposure provides brilliant, grape-ripening sun. These hillsides above the Rhône River can reach a gradient of 55 degrees; the picturesque, terraced vineyards, first cultivated during the Roman era, produce a wine celebrated for its perfume and longevity, attracting the notice of connoisseurs from Pliny to Thomas Jefferson. Along with Hermitage, some twenty miles to the south, Côte-Rôtie is the ultimate terroir for Syrah, which may be indigenous, although this is a matter of hot dispute in ampelographical circles. I think of Côte-Rôtie as Fitzgerald to Hermitage's Hemingway; like Fitzgerald's, Côte-Rôtie's reputation was almost moribund at mid-century. The steep, rocky hillside vineyards require punishing manual labor, and after the Second World War many vintners abandoned the vines and planted apricots.

Any wine that can somehow harmonize the flavors of raspberry and bacon—not to mention aromas like violet and leather—is worth saving, in my book. The white knight in this story is Marcel Guigal, heir to the firm that his father established in 1946. Traditionally, the wines of Côte-Rôtie depended on a blend from different parcels all over the hillside to achieve complexity and balance. The sandy limestone soils of the southerly Côte Blonde are supposed to provide finesse; those of the larger Côte Brune, with more clay and iron, breed power and longevity. Guigal began bottling his finest parcels separately, starting with the vineyards La Mouline and La Landonne and, later, La Turque. He aged these wines in 100 percent new oak barrels for as long as forty-two months. When Robert Parker started raving about these new-wave Côte-Rôties and giving them 100 point ratings, the wine world sat up and drooled. They are now among the most prized—and expensive—wines on the planet, and their fame has rubbed off on their neighbors.

Still, the Guigal wines were controversial; romantics complained that the taste of new oak masked the distinctive characteristics of Côte-Rôtie. Importer and author Kermit Lynch, who praises traditional Côte-Rôtie for its seductive combination of vigor and delicacy (blonde and brunette), complained that Guigal produces "an inky, oaky, monster." He finds it ironic that the appellation has been saved from desuetude by a wine that is freakishly uncharacteristic. Lynch has a point, though it has to be said that traditional Côte-Rôtie vinification too often resulted in nasty flavors from old, unsanitary barrels and green flavors from stems. And I have to admit that I'm a slut for a good vintage of La Mouline or La Turque. Over the past decade, others have emulated Guigal: Yves Gangloff, Jean-Michel Gerin, Delas Frères, Tardieu-Laurent, and the Hermitage firm of Chapoutier are producing big, modern Syrahs. But the largest group, exemplified by the domaine of René Rostaing, has struck a balance between the old and new styles. In fact, a kind of counterreformation has recently begun—some of the new Young Turks are pragmatists who talk a lot about tradition and finesse.

A bullet-headed man of solid build and military demeanor, Eric Texier made a big splash among American oenophiles with his debut vintage '99 Côte-Rôtie. (Curiously, 95 percent of his wine is exported.) A native of the Bordeaux region and a former nuclear engineer, Texier first traveled to Oregon and California to get a New World perspective. He became fascinated with the Rhône region, and started studying the nineteenth-century literature in order to determine the best vineyard sites. Texier uses 40 percent new oak in his lush, elegant Côte-Rôtie, which always showcases the signature Côte-Rôtie taste of raspberry.

The father-and-son team of Michel and Stephane Ogier is similarly pragmatic. Until 1980, Michel sold his grapes to negotiants, including Guigal. Now, he and twenty-four-year-old Stephane, who towers over his wiry, balding father and looks a lot like Brendan Fraser, produce several seductive estate-bottled Côte-Rôties using a combination of traditional and new techniques. Another rising star of the appellation is Texier's former friend Pierre Gaillard, a gregarious, good-natured man whose fingernails are as dirty as any of the local farmers', although he is a well-traveled cosmopolitan who likes to debate the merits of Opus One versus Margaux. (He prefers the former.) Gaillard worked as vineyard manager at the old firm Vidal-Fleury, where he planted the famed La Turque vineyard. He worked for Guigal after it bought Vidal-Fleury, and eventually began to purchase his own vineyard parcels, the most prized of which, Côte Rozier, produced one of the best wines of the 2000 vintage. Other makers to look for are Burgaud, Clusel-Roch, Jamet, Bernard Levet, and—my desert-island Côte-Rôtie—Jasmin.

Côte-Rôtie typically takes five to ten years to show its potential (and shed that nasty young Syrah burnt-rubber smell). As for recent vintages, 2001 was classic, while the superhot 2003 wines are more massive and voluptuous and roasted. The 2005 may prove superior to both. Côte-Rôtie is one of the smallest appellations in France, and the output is minuscule. Guigal's Côte-Rôtie Brune et Blonde is the only wine made in enough quantity to appear at retail outlets throughout the country. Most other Côte-Rôties take work to find and are best reserved in advance. The following importer-retailers are among the best sources. You should be on their mailing lists.

North Berkeley Imports, 1601 Martin Luther King Jr. Way, Berkeley, CA 94709; 800-266-6585; northberkeley imports.com. (Texier and Gaillard)

Kermit Lynch Wine Merchant, 1605 San Pablo Ave., Berkeley, CA 94702; 510-524-1524; kermitlynch.com; fax: 510-528-7026. (Jasmin, Rostaing)

Sam's Wines & Spirits, 1720 N. Marcey St., Chicago, IL 60614; 800-777-9137; samswine.com. (Chapoutier, Gerin, Burgaud, others)

Rosenthal Wine Merchant, 318 E. 84th St., New York, NY 10028; 212-249-6650. (Cuilleron, Bernard Levet)

THE HOUSE RED OF THE MONTAGUES

AND THE CAPULETS

When über-restaurateur Danny Meyer entertained his child-hood idol, St. Louis Cardinals right-hander Bob Gibson, he thought long and hard about what wine to serve to the pitcher, whom he knew to be a serious oenophile. Gibson had arrived at Meyer's Gramercy Park apartment with a bottle of Turley Cellars Hayne Vineyard Zinfandel, a big purple Hummer of a wine that's always a hard act to follow. Meyer, whose restaurants, such as Gramercy Tavern and Union Square Cafe, are known for having some of the best wine lists in the country, finally decided on a 1990 Quintarelli Recioto della Valpolicella. Gibson must have been pleased. I know I was ecstatic when Meyer brought the second of his three cherished bottles to my apartment recently for dinner; it was probably the best wine I've had this year.

Okay, I can hear some of you snickering out there. It's true that Valpolicella has pretty much the same image problem in this country as Soave, which is no coincidence, since the two regions adjoin each other and the same giant corporation has been shipping vast quantities of bland Valpolicella and Soave to this country since the 1970s. For some of us, the wine is a part of our history that we'd rather forget, a name associated with dim memories of embarrassing dates—like certain hairstyles from the era of Foreigner and Leo Sayer. But anybody who has recently tasted a Valpolicella from Quintarelli or dal Forno has a different impression.

Quintarelli and dal Forno are the Plato and Aristotle of Valpolicella, and the legitimate question is whether they are superfreaks who happen to make great wine here or whether they are pioneers in a region that is catching up to them. Romano dal Forno's father and grandfather made Valpolicella on their small family estate, but dal Forno says that he knew virtually nothing about wine until he met Giuseppe Quintarelli, the genial genius who lived a couple of valleys away near the town of Negrar, back in 1981. "He basically adopted me," the stocky and intense dal Forno told me when I visited him last year. Dal Forno speaks about wine as if it were a matter of life and death: "I tried to absorb everything." He seems to have succeeded. His Valpolicellas are more intense than most Amarones, and his Amarones should be opened only in the presence of gods and stinky cheeses.

The Valpolicella region encompasses a series of picturesque north-south ridges that are often described as resembling the fingers of an open hand. The dominant red grape here is Corvina, which shares the hillsides with cherry trees. Valpolicella is the hometown red in Verona, the ancient city that Romeo and Juliet made famous, which has lately become the setting for Vinitaly, a gigantic trade fair that fills the hotels and ties up the streets every March. The two-story "booth" of the Valpolicella-based Allegrini winery is literally and figuratively the biggest thing at the fair. But just as Valpolicella is starting to get sexy, it's also getting a little complicated. We're starting to hear the phrase "super-Valpolicellas," and some of the most interesting wines from the region don't even carry the V-word on their label. The Recioto della Valpolicella mentioned above is a sweet version, made from dried grapes. And some dry Valpolicellas are turbocharged with dried grape skins left over from the production of Recioto, a method known as *ripasso*. Got that?

Probably the easiest way to understand the wines of Valpolicella is to think of a continuum between the lightest and the richest. On the lightest end of the scale are wines labeled simply Valpolicella, like the notorious Bolla (which is improving under American ownership). At the other end of the scale are Recioto della Valpolicella, produced from grapes that are dried on mats for three or four months after the harvest in order to concentrate the sugars before fermenting, and Amarone, its dry cousin, made by the same process, except that the grapes are allowed to ferment until the sugar is gone.

Amarone—or, to use its full name, Amarone della Valpolicella—was the first wine from the Valpolicella appellation to get respect. But in recent years the quality and the reputation of ordinary Valpolicella have improved as well. "The wines used to stink," says Sergio Esposito of New York's Italian Wine Merchants. "Literally—they smelled like feet." Esposito suggests that just as Barolo producers started to pay attention to the quality of their Barberas and Dolcettos in the 1990s, the top Amarone producers are boosting the quality of their dry reds with lower yields and improved cellar work. Allegrini has all but abandoned the appellation name, turning out some brilliant Corvina-based wines under the names La Grola, Palazzo della Torre, and La Poja.

Valpolicellas that have been turbocharged by the *ripasso* method (usually indicated on the label) can taste like junior Amarones, with hints of tar, leather, dates, and figs, and can stand up to a grilled rib eye or lamb chops. The Reciotos make a tremendous accompaniment to a cheese plate. But don't overlook the simpler pleasures of a good Valpolicella Superiore—with an obligatory 12 percent alcohol and at least a year of aging—from makers like Brigaldara, Nicolis, Tedeschi, and Zenato, which typically sells for about fifteen dollars. Any one of these might become your new house red.

"AN EXTREME, EMOTIONAL WINE"

Amarone

"Amarone is an extreme wine," Romano dal Forno warns, pausing as we descend the spiral staircase of his villa to the chilly depths of the wine cellar, where I'm suddenly struck by how much he looks like a weather-beaten version of James Gandolfini. "It's an emotional wine," he continues. For a moment, I wonder if he's implying that I may not be man enough for the job ahead. After sampling several vintages from the barrel, I'm indeed a little emotional—exhilarated and also saddened by the knowledge that, rare and expensive as it is, I will seldom taste dal Forno's radical juice again.

Amarone is an anomaly: a dry wine that mimics sweetness; a relatively modern creation that seems deeply primitive and rustic, like some kind of rich pagan nectar or the blood of a mythological beast. While Italians consider food and wine to be inseparable, Amarone overwhelms most dishes. "With Amarone, you don't think about food," dal Forno says. "Cheese, maybe."

Dal Forno is the most extreme proponent of this extreme red, made from dried grapes—mostly Corvina—in the Valpolicella hills outside Verona. His turbocharged Amarones, produced only in the better vintages, tip the scales above 15 percent alcohol and make most cult Cabernets seem dainty by comparison. In the past decade, thanks to Robert Parker, dal Forno's wines have become as revered as those of his mentor, Giuseppe Quintarelli, with whom he worked before assuming responsibility for his father's vineyards.

Quintarelli's estate sits in the hills of the Valpolicella Classico region, at the end of a long driveway lined with meticulously pruned olive trees—holy ground for the wine geek. Sticking his head out the window in answer to my repeated ringing of his doorbell, the resident saint sports a large bib across his green herringbone jacket and a smear of tomato sauce on his chin. A genial baldie in his seventies, Quintarelli seems to have no recollection of our appointment but cheerfully agrees to show me around after he has finished lunch and, presumably, the game show that is blaring in the background.

Quintarelli's cellar is pleasingly cluttered and medieval-looking, full of giant old Slovenian casks. I don't see any steel tanks. Nor any of the new oak barriques that dominate dal Forno's pristine cellar. Although the family resemblance is unmistakable, Quintarelli's Amarones are more earthy than dal Forno's, and even more complex, suggestive of figs and dates, bittersweet cherry and black licorice. They inspire contemplation and wonder. To my mind, they are the ultimate expression of this extreme concept. My visit overlaps with that of two French wine writers whose initial irritation at sharing the cellar with an American is eventually overridden by their pleasure in the wine, which they acknowledge is unlike anything produced in la belle France.

The courtly, tweedy Stefano Cesari, proprietor of the

nearby Brigaldara estate, shows me the real secret of Amarone, leading me up a flight of stairs to a loft in the barn behind his fourteenth-century villa, where thousands of wooden trays are suspended, one atop another. If most wines are made in the cellar, Amarone is made in the attic.

Every fall, the choicest grapes of the vintage are set out in racks to dry for a period of months. This process, which dates back at least to the time of Pliny, who commended it, concentrates the sugar—and often induces botrytis, the noble rot responsible for the flavor of the great whites of Sauternes. (Botrytis is not welcomed by all makers; some, like Allegrini, have installed humidity-controlled drying chambers to prevent its formation.) Drying does for the grapes what a turbocharger does for a V-8 engine. Traditionally, a sweet wine resulted, because the grapes stopped fermenting before the sugar was consumed. Called Recioto della Valpolicella, this sweet red is still produced. Cesari tells me the first cask of Amarone was a mistake—a barrel that fermented all the way to dryness sometime in the early part of the century (other sources point to much earlier origins). This style became known as amaro (bitter) recioto and was eventually produced in commercial quantities in the 1950s.

Just as its exact origins are obscure, Amarone remains a mysterious, almost schizophrenic wine. As Bastianich and Lynch suggest in *Vino Italiano*, "It behaves like a sweet wine without technically being sweet." The bouquet of dried fruits and the syrupy texture suggest port; it tends to trick the palate by seeming sweet in the beginning and finishing dry, even slightly bitter, like unsweetened chocolate.

When I get in the Amarone mood, I often look for Allegrini, one of the most innovative and exciting estates in Valpolicella, or Brigaldara, which excelled not only in the stellar '97 vintage but also in the less opulent '98 and '99 vintages. Bussola, Masi, and Tedeschi make powerhouse Amarones in the dal Forno mold, while Accordini, Bertani, Bolla (yup, that Bolla), and Speri produce slightly lighter, more approachable versions.

As complex as it is, I like to think of Amarone as the perfect primer wine for those who are suspicious of the cornucopia of flavor analogies that wine critics come up with. I'm often baffled myself when I read wine notes full of huckleberries and hawthorn blossoms. But give me a glass of Amarone and I'm the man! Step back, Bob Parker! Even the beginning taster can feel like a professional as he effortlessly identifies the intense flavors and aromas of the most extreme red wine on the planet. Cherries! Dates! Figs! Black licorice! Leather! Coffee! Bittersweet chocolate! Tobacco! Et cetera, et cetera.

CAPE CRUSADERS

South African Reds

Nelson Mandela, Charlize Theron, and Pinotage are among South Africa's distinctive contributions to global culture. The last is an unlikely hybrid of two French grape varietals: finicky, noble Pinot Noir and mulish Cinsault—imagine the love child of Jean Seberg and Congressman Bob Barr. Who knows what Professor Abraham Perold was drinking when he came up with this idea. While Pinotage can sometimes smell like nail polish remover au poivre, at its best it improves with age and is actually capable of provoking contemplative enjoyment.

The best way to see if you're fond of Pinotage is to look for a bottle from Kanonkop, a winery located in Stellenbosch. (I assume the name has something to do with the seventeenth-century cannon that greets you at the end of the driveway of this beautiful estate.) Kanonkop is to Pinotage what Petrarch is to the sonnet, although the winery also makes a very good Bordeaux-style blend, which has twice won France's Pichon Longueville Comtesse de Lalande trophy. These victories suggest that South African reds have arrived on the international scene, but the news has been slow to reach these shores.

For several years now my favorite South African red has been the Pinot Noir from Hamilton Russell Vineyards, a hillside estate in the Walker Bay region, less than two miles from the Indian Ocean. A relative newcomer in a country whose wine history spans almost four hundred years, the property was established in 1976 by Tim Hamilton Russell, who struggled tirelessly against restrictive and irrational regulations; it's now run by his son Anthony, an Oxford-educated whirling dervish who likes to say he's just a farmer, although I've observed firsthand that he cuts a very stylish figure on dance floors from Cape Town to Manhattan.

The cool microclimate of this area, with its marauding baboons and its clay soil studded with prehistoric hand axes, produces the most Burgundian New World Pinot I've ever tasted, with the kind of earthiness, complexity, and age-worthiness rarely found outside Burgundy. The neighboring estate of Bouchard Finlayson, started by Hamilton Russell's former winemaker, is also producing fine Pinot, as is newcomer Flagstone, a winery to watch for its Pinotage and blends as well.

Cabernet and Bordeaux blends are currently attracting the lion's share of capital and energy, and the warmer region of Stellenbosch is probably the top appellation for these wines. It's also among the most dramatic landscapes I've ever seen, where green valleys with white stucco Cape Dutch farmhouses could almost pass for Flemish landscapes, except that they are framed by jagged, vertiginous gray mountain ridges. The pioneer of Bordeaux-style wines in the Cape is Meerlust, an estate more than three hundred years old that makes earthy, slow-maturing reds, including a Merlot, and its standard-bearer, Rubicon (not to be confused with Francis

Coppola's wine of the same name). Another historic Stellenbosch estate, a few kilometers up the road, Rustenburg is producing serious, curranty Cabernet blends that are drawing international interest. Nearby, Rust en Vrede makes rich, powerful Cabernet, Shiraz, and Merlot, and, finally, an estate wine that is a blend of all three—which seems to be the new Cape trend. None of these wines will cost as much as a good *cru bourgeois* Bordeaux from the 2003 vintage.

Rupert & Rothschild, in the adjacent Paarl appellation, is a joint venture between one of South Africa's wealthiest families and the Baron Edmond branch of the Rothschilds from France. Until his death in a car accident, it was run by Anthonij Rupert, the gruff, Charles Barkley–sized black sheep of the family. This historic estate is producing very good Cab blends, with the help of Pomerol's ubiquitous Michel Rolland. Rupert sometimes took longer than his wines to show his charming side, but I spent a hugely entertaining day with him, talking about wine, Italian tailoring, and African wildlife after turning into his driveway unannounced, and I was saddened to hear of his death. The winemaking continues to be in the capable hands of Schalk-Willem Joubert and Rolland. Another deep-pocketed venture producing Bordeaux-style blends is Vergelegen, owned by hydra-headed Anglo-American Industries. Winemaker André van Rensburg, hired a few years back, comes with a reputation as a serious Shiraz specialist, and is planting plenty of this varietal, which is gaining ground in South Africa, as everywhere else. In fact, I suspect that Cabernet-Shiraz blends may have a big and delicious future in the Cape.

Of the many hours I have spent lost on back roads of wine regions around the world, I doubt if I ever felt more lost in the wilderness than I did looking for the property of pro golfer David Frost in the remote foothills of Paarl. Frost gives lousy directions, but his Cabernet is a big currant bomb, and he is what the South Africans call a rugger bugger and what we would call a good old boy—a generous and gregarious host despite the fact that he was feeling the effects of a long night with his good friend Anthonij Rupert the night before. After the long hangover from apartheid-era isolation, South Africa's red wines, like its actresses and golfers, are ready to compete internationally.

When the estate of the late Bill Blass was auctioned by Sotheby's, I couldn't help wondering about the fate of a certain item—a medal he had received at a ceremony in New York inducting him into the Confrères des Chevaliers du Cahors some five or six years ago. I was also inducted into the society that night, though, like Blass, I was slightly baffled by the honor, and hardly knew where Cahors was at the time. I have since visited the region and sampled many of its wines, and when I drink the big wines of Cahors I often think of Blass, a big man who exuded a hypermasculine sense of personal style.

Cahors is butch. Peter the Great was one of its many admirers, and his enthusiasm was shared by his countrymen. The "black wine" of Cahors was renowned for its power and density and was sometimes used to punch up the wimpier reds of Bordeaux. This muscular, tannic red wine of Cahors developed alongside the hearty, fatty cuisine of the southwest: foie gras, cassoulet, confit, and maigret de canard.

From the Middle Ages until the middle of the nineteenth century the reds of Cahors were as famous as any in Europe, until phylloxera wiped out the vineyards. When initial attempts to graft the local Auxerrois vines onto disease-resistant American rootstocks failed, many growers planted hybrids that produced insipid *vins ordinaires*. By the middle of this century the big inky drink that was *le vrai* Cahors was almost extinct.

After devastating frosts in 1956 and 1957, a Cahors native named José Baudel left his post as the head of the government research center in Bordeaux to take over the local cooperative wine cellar and to save the wine of his homeland from oblivion. Baudel worked to banish the hybrids and propagate Auxerrois (known elsewhere as Malbec), a tannic grape that seems to have a particular affinity for the soils and climate of the Lot River Valley and the adjacent plateau.

In the last decade Cahors has made a comeback, as its winemakers groped to integrate their traditions with new technology and the international marketplace. "Ten years ago there was a midlife crisis," says Ariane Daguin, proprietor of D'Artagan in New York, which specializes in the cuisine of her native region. "The wines, which had evolved in symbiosis with that heavy cuisine, were big and tannic. When people started eating lighter, they had to learn to lighten them up a little." That said, Cahors will never be a dainty, aperitif kind of drink. It will never make a nice accompaniment for a plate of steamed vegetables, nor should it go to the beach. But it ought to find favor with advocates of high-fat, high-protein diets à la Atkins.

Locals consider Cahors to be the logical accompaniment to foie gras, and to most dishes involving black truffles— Cahors being more or less the heart of the Périgord region. The preternaturally boyish Pierre-Jean Pebeyre is a fourth-generation truffle negotiant; dining with Pebeyre and his wife,

Babethe, in the town of Cahors I have experienced some stunning food-and-wine pairings involving black truffles and Cahors. The Pebeyres taught me to make a sauce of butter whisked into warm truffle juice (available in tins) with pureed black truffles, which eroticizes almost any simple dish.

Stendahl once remarked on the resemblance of this part of France to Tuscany, and as in Chianti, the wine story here is partly one of deep-pocketed outsiders coming in to reinvigorate the area. Alain Senderens, proprietor-chef of three-star Lucas Carton in Paris, bought Château Gautoul in 1992.

The hyperactive Alain Dominique Perrin, former president of Cartier, who bought Château Lagrézette, with its impressive fifteenth-century château, in 1980, has become the Robert Mondavi of the region, the chief promoter and innovator of Cahors. Perrin seems to know nearly everyone of interest on the planet and has the photos in the château to prove it. His luxury cuvée Le Pigeonnier has set a new standard, with high ratings and a price to match. The superconcentration and 100 percent new oak treatment make this wine seem almost as international and polished as its proprietor, as if it were wearing a Cartier Panther watch around its neck; but in some ways I prefer the regular cuvée of Lagrézette, which seems more distinctively regional and less like something that could have come from Australia.

Alain Gayraud, the wildly enthusiastic proprietor of Lamartine, at the western edge of the appellation, still uses the cement fermentation tanks his grandfather built, and employs new oak barrels sparingly. His wines are among the most distinctive I encountered in my visit, muscular but a little reserved, requiring time to reveal their considerable charms and distinctive regional character. Gayraud makes three different cuvées, the lesser of which is more accessible on release, as does nearby Domaine Pineraie, where they've been making wine continuously since 1456. Among the domaines worth looking for are Châteaux du Cèdre, Clos Triguedina, Croix de Mayne, Haute-Serre, and Château Peche de Jammes, owned by Americans Sherry and Stephen Schechter.

As with Bordeaux, the vintages to seek out are the 2000, the 2003, and the 2005. Although these wines will be decidedly young and somewhat wild, they should behave well in the company of a cassoulet or a charred slab of prime beef.

Giuseppe Rivetti, the proprietor of La Spinetta, describes Barbera as "the anti-Merlot"—which is as good a starting point as any other for a discussion of this provincial grape with multiple personalities. It's easier to say what it isn't than what it is. I take Rivetti's comment to mean that Barbera is not the kind of mellow international beverage you order by the glass at the bar of a revolving cocktail lounge while listening to a pianist cover Billy Joel. Certainly Rivetti's Barberas, with their rustic exuberance and feisty acidity, are more likely to evoke a noisy trattoria redolent of roasted goat.

The poor relation of noble Nebbiolo, Barbera had long been the workhorse of Piedmont, accounting for half of the region's red-wine production. Barbera ripens earlier than the fussy Nebbiolo, the grape used in Barolo and Barbaresco, and was traditionally planted on cooler slopes and lesser sites. (The dirty little secret of Piedmont is that Barbera was—and, many say, still is—added to Barolo and Barbaresco to boost the color and add body.) Barbera typically produced a rustic plonk that was acidic enough to stand up to tomato sauce. Insofar as it was known outside the region, it was known as a pizza wine. Lacking in natural tannins—which extend the life of red wines—it was meant to be consumed young, and often.

A few wistful growers had Cinderella visions for this local grape. They wondered if, with the proper upbringing, it might not be capable of stardom. What if it was raised on prime real estate? What if it went to finishing school to learn French? Angelo Gaja, who revolutionized the treatment of Nebbiolo, told me recently that he was the first person to experiment with Barbera and French oak barrels back in 1969—the wood supplying the tannins that were missing from the grape itself. The idea was also proposed by French oenologist Émile Peynaud, who was consulting for a winery in Asti in the early 1970s. By most accounts, the man who actually placed the glass slipper on Cinderella's foot was the late Giacomo Bologna, a motorcycle-riding, jazz-loving, barrel-chested bon vivant.

A native of sleepy Rocchetta Tanaro, some ten miles east of the town of Asti, Bologna inherited a property called Braida and experimented with practices that seemed radical at the time. He planted Barbera on prime, sun-drenched slopes; picked the grapes late, to alleviate some of their acidity; and aged the juice in toasted new French oak barrels, which further softened the hard edges while lending the wine some wood tannins, giving it more structure. In 1982, the same year that changed the face of Bordeaux, Bologna created Bricco dell'Uccellone, a barrel-aged, vineyard-designated Barbera that rapidly caught the attention of the international wine world, and of Bologna's neighbors. Bricco was the first super-Barbera. Call it Barbarella. (They're big on nicknames in the Piedmont. L'Uccellone is named for the crowlike old woman who used to own the vineyard; *l'uselun* means big bird.)

More than two decades after Bologna created this new,

sophisticated, smoking-jacket style of Barbera, it's hard to generalize about this grape except to say that quality is better at all levels. Barbera is as stylistically all over the map as Zinfandel, another blending grape that has achieved recent renown. Many makers continue to produce the lighter-style Barbera—which can be a tremendous value, particularly given the recent string of stellar vintages in Piedmont. The 2000, 2001, and 2003 vintages all achieved a ripeness that should counterbalance the natural acidity of the grape; good examples, like Michele Chiarlo's Barbera d'Asti Superiore and Icardi's Barbera d'Asti Tabarin, retail for about fifteen dollars. Barbera d'Asti is often fatter and fruitier than Barbera d'Alba, in part because the best, sunniest slopes in Alba are reserved for Nebbiolo, producing Barolo and Barbaresco. Many of the greatest producers of Barolo—Scavino, Clerico, Mascarello, Sandrone, and Aldo and Giacomo Conterno, among others—make supple, sophisticated Barbera d'Alba at a fraction of the price. The most concentrated, powerful Barberas are usually identified by vineyard name—often involving some variation of the word *bric*, which means hilltop in the local dialect. Price is another key indicator—the Barbarellas, like Franco Martinetti's powerful Montruc, can sell for upwards of fifty dollars.

Bricco dell'Uccellone has proven itself over the past two decades to be a serious, ageworthy wine. Tasting at the winery this past spring with Raffaella and Giuseppe, Giacomo Bologna's children, I was deeply impressed by the complexity and freshness of the '89 and '90 Bricco dell'Uccellone. The '01 is another classic. The Bologna family makes several other excellent Barberas, including Bricco della Bigotta and Ai

Suma. The most mind-boggling Barberas I've tasted recently were from La Spinetta, which in 2001 was named winery of the year in the Italian wine bible *Gambero Rosso*. My teeth are still stained from the experience of tasting the '99 Barbera d'Alba Gallina and the '99 Barbera d'Asti that spring; both reminded me in some ways of great, old-vine Zinfandels, and also reminded me of a blackberry fight I had with two fifth-grade classmates in Vancouver, Canada. We were picking blackberries, and after we'd filled two buckets and eaten several handfuls, we started throwing the surplus at one another. Thirty years later, Giuseppe Rivetti's Barberas made me almost that exuberant.

GO ASK ALICE

The Dark Secret of Bandol

Many of you fashionable diners and sophisticated travelers are probably familiar with the refreshing, slightly bitter rosés of Bandol. From West Hollywood to Sardinia, Domaine Ott rosé is the official summertime beverage of the Prada and Hermès brigades. But fewer are aware that Bandol—a middle-class resort and fishing town between Marseille and Toulon—is home to one of the world's great red wines.

"Bandol rouge has been the love of my life," says Alice Waters, one of the great epicures of our time. Indeed, Domaine Tempier rouge has been more or less the house wine at Chez Panisse, in Berkeley, since it opened, some thirty years ago. "They have incredibly long lives and incredible perfume," Waters says of red Bandols. "I can always pick them out blind in a tasting." Waters particularly likes them with lamb, strong cheese, and figs. "And a young one slightly chilled can be incredible with bouillabaisse."

I would add dry-rubbed spare ribs and beef stew to this list.

"Kind of like a cross between Barolo, Brunello, and Châteauneuf-du-Pape" is how Will Helburn of Rosenthal Wine Merchant describes red Bandol. Like Châteauneuf-du-Pape, it is the product of hot Provençal summers, redolent of the wild herbs (known collectively as *garrigue*) that perfume the hillsides, and probably best appreciated in the cooler months, alongside red meat or wild game. Like Barolo or Brunello, it is stubborn, sulky, and slow to evolve, which may account for its wallflower status.

Two centuries ago, Bandol reds were ranked alongside those of Bordeaux and Burgundy and were prized for their longevity—a quality attributable to the Mourvèdre grape, which is highly resistant to oxidation. However, the vineyards of Provence were replanted with higher-yielding and less-demanding grape varieties after phylloxera wiped out the Mourvèdre late in the nineteenth century, and Bandol never really recovered its luster.

The story of Bandol's resurrection is murkier than a fermenting barrel sample of young Mourvèdre. (Importer Kermit Lynch, who owns a house in the region, recounts at least two and a half different versions in his classic book *Adventures on the Wine Route*.) All that need concern us here is that two or three determined growers worked together to restore the noble Mourvèdre to the hillsides and set strict regulations for the appellation.

"Bandol is about Mourvèdre," says Neal Rosenthal, who imports one of the finest—Château Pradeaux. While the regulations allow up to 50 percent Grenache and Cinsault, the best wines are mostly Mourvèdre. When young, Bandol Mourvèdre tastes like ripe blackberries squashed up with old tea bags. With age, after growing up in a microbiologically active cellar in Provence, it can smell like old sweaty saddle leather, dry-aged beef, and even wet fur. And I mean that as a compliment.

Fans of the increasingly expensive great Châteauneuf of Château de Beaucastel will probably love Pibarnon, Pradeaux, or Tempier—three of the top Bandols. Beaucastel is about 30 percent Mourvèdre, and like the other three is made without new oak, which can mask flavors and aromas. Fans of clean, technically perfect, tutti-frutti New World winemaking may well be horrified by the slightly funky herbal characteristics of a great aged Bandol. If you're the kind of person who would never consider sharing a room with a wet Labrador retriever or a lit cigar, then I advise you to skip the rest of this column.

Like Nebbiolo, Mourvèdre is a late-ripening, tannic grape that doesn't do well much north of the Mediterranean. "Mourvèdre needs to smell the sea," claims poetic Randall Grahm of Bonny Doon Vineyard, who has made some fine California versions of Bandol rouge.

Château Pradeaux is a mere three-iron away from the Mediterranean. The vineyard has been in the Portalis family since before the French Revolution, and the big, gamy, backward wines made there may well resemble those of the nineteenth century—what the French call *les vins de garde*. Hold the saliva for a couple of decades; Rosenthal is just now uncorking his '82s, while waiting for the monster '89s and '90s to open up. Not exactly a wine for instant gratification, but worth the wait. "You can actually smell the sun," says Rosenthal of a mature Pradeaux. "Beeswax and tiger lilies are the high notes, animal fur and saddle leather underneath."

A little farther from the ocean, Domaine Tempier is a relatively recent creation. As part of his dowry upon his marriage to Lulu Tempier, Lucien Peyraud received several hectares of neglected vines in the hills outside Bandol. By all accounts one of the great personalities of the past century, Peyraud started researching the history of the area and replanting the vineyards with Mourvèdre. By the time he died, he had created a great domaine and a global cult of aficionados for his bold, long-lived reds and his carpe diem rosés—a tradition that continues with his sons François and Jean-Marie. A few years back I shared a bottle of truffly, rosemary- and Montecristo-scented 1969 with Kermit Lynch in the cellar of the domaine and guessed it to be fifteen years younger.

Other excellent Bandols include Domaines Bunan and Château La Rouvière. Prices are generally lower than for Châteauneuf-du-Pape or Barolo. No one would be happier than I to see them remain so. On the other hand, development pressure in the area is so fierce that increasing renown and prices for the wines of Bandol may be the only hope for preserving some of these beautiful hillside vineyards.

I once speculated that the grapes for a certain luxury Champagne were harvested individually, by vestal virgins, never suspecting that I would one day witness something close to this whimsical vision. Arriving at the winery of Casa Lapostolle in Chile's Colchagua Valley one morning in March, I encountered some ninety women lined up on either side of a narrow table about the length of a tennis court, plucking Cabernet grapes one by one from dewy clusters that were handpicked that morning, saving the best and discarding those that were damaged or unripe. High-end winemakers around the world employ sorting tables and manual labor to roughly edit out the leaves from the clusters, but I've never seen it done literally grape by grape. The grapes in question were destined for the winery's Clos Apalta, one of Chile's new wave of luxury reds. The radically meticulous sorting process was one more piece of evidence, if I needed it, that Chilean wine is not just for swilling anymore.

Chile's Central Valley—located in the center of this tall, skinny country, and crisscrossed by rivers and subvalleys—is a paradise for grapes. The climate, moderated by the Andes to the east and the Pacific to the west, is often described as being a cross between those of Napa and Bordeaux. Wine grapes arrived with the missionaries who followed the conquistadors, and the importation of vines (and winemakers) from France in the mid-nineteenth century created an invaluable viticultural resource; what never arrived in Chile was phylloxera, the disease that subsequently devastated most of the world's vineyards. The raw material was in place, although it remained underexploited until the end of the Pinochet era, when domestic wineries began to look to the international market and foreign wine interests started pouring money into the Central Valley.

Alexandra Marnier-Lapostolle, whose great-grandfather invented Grand Marnier, began scouting Chile in the early 1990s and then brought in Michel Rolland, the renowned and ubiquitous oenologist. In 1994 she and her husband, Cyril de Bournet, founded Casa Lapostolle and secured Rolland's services as a consultant. As you follow her through a dusty vineyard while she tastes grapes and talks about prephylloxera rootstocks, you keep thinking that Lapostolle is one of those chic, svelte, and devastatingly attractive women you see on the rue du Faubourg Saint-Honoré. It seems appropriate that she describes Clos Apalta as her "haute couture wine." (Lapostolle also produces two lines in the ten- to twenty-dollar range.) The grapes, which are so tenderly plucked at the winery, come from a nearly hundred-year-old vineyard of gnarled Cabernet, Merlot, and Carmenère vines in the Colchagua Valley, which is bounded by a horseshoe of snowcapped mountains.

Carmenère is Chile's secret weapon, a varietal once widespread in Bordeaux that in 1991 was rediscovered in Chile, where for years it had been mistaken for Merlot. Like Cabernet Franc, Carmenère can be a little vegetal and rustic, but when properly ripened it has a silky texture and peppery, raspberry flavor. Whether it can be a solo star for Chile's wine industry remains to be seen, but the spectacular Clos Apalta, which contains up to 40 percent Carmenère, is testament enough to this grape's potential as a blending component. The monster 2001 Apalta is already a wine-world legend; the 2002 is slightly less powerful but just as complex, a wine that might be mistaken for a blend of a Napa cult Cab and a first-growth Pauillac.

Seña, a joint venture between Napa's Robert Mondavi and Eduardo Chadwick, president of the venerable Chilean winery Errázuriz, was the first of the superpremium (i.e., fifty dollars plus) Chilean reds, and is likewise a blend of Cabernet, Merlot, and Carmenère. The New World–style 2001 vintage is the finest offspring of this marriage to date. If any Chilean winery can claim more distinguished bloodlines, it would be Almaviva, the love child of Bordeaux's Baron Philippe de Rothschild (Mondavi's Opus One partner) and Chile's Concha y Toro, the first winery to be listed on the New York Stock Exchange. The monumental 2001 Almaviva, made by Mouton-Rothschild's Patrick Léon with Enrique Tirado of Concha y Toro, tastes a lot like a fine Pauillac—a structured (read: slow to evolve), complex, and earthy blend of roughly 80 percent Cabernet Sauvignon and 20 percent Carmenère. The grapes come from a thirty-year-old vineyard located on the outskirts of Santiago in the Maipo Valley, Chile's traditional Cabernet region; they undergo their miraculous transubstantiation in a beautiful wooden cathedral of a winery designed by Chilean architect Martín Hurtado Covarrubias, best known for his churches.

The young prodigy among Chile's homegrown wineries is unquestionably Montes, founded in 1988. Montes Alpha "M" is the flagship wine of the estate, a rich, powerful red made from relatively young vines planted on hillsides above the Apalta Valley in Colchagua. My pick for the most promising of Chile's newer estates is Haras de Pirque, in the Maipo Valley, best known at present for its Thoroughbred stud farm. Founded in 1991 by entrepreneur-equestrian Eduardo Matte, Haras currently produces a Cabernet aptly named Elegance and has recently announced a joint-venture, single-vineyard wine with Italy's Antinori family.

Most of these new-wave Chilean luxury cuvées are as yet made only in small quantities, but they are worth seeking out, and they bode well for Chile's future as a source of premium reds. Seventy or eighty dollars may seem like a lot to pay for a Chilean wine—until you compare the best of them with similarly priced New World reds.

MALBEC RISING

I hear that South America is coming into style.
—Elvis Costello

Argentinean Malbec may not quite rank with the tango and the collected works of Jorge Luis Borges as a cultural landmark, but at this point I'd judge it a not-too-distant third—particularly when it is served alongside the fire-grilled, grass-fed beef of the pampas. To experience this combination among the svelte, stylish, late-dining patrons of La Cabaña in Buenos Aires, or better yet at an *asado*—a traditional outdoor barbecue—in the lean, limpid air of the high Andes, is to flirt with some kind of primordial carnivore bliss.

With its tragic, underachieving history and its malfunctioning political and economic institutions, Argentina is years behind neighboring Chile as a producer of world-class wines. But its natural endowments and its potential are probably greater. And while grape varieties like Cabernet Sauvignon and Chardonnay thrive on the arid plateaus of the Andes' eastern flanks, Malbec—unloved and almost forgotten in its homeland of southwestern France—seems to have found its perfect adoptive home here. Not to mention its perfect foil in Argentinean beef.

Argentina is a vegetarian's worst nightmare. Salads can be

found in the fashionable restaurants of Buenos Aires, and good French- and Italian-style pastry is widely available, but, generally speaking, beef—with a smattering of pork and lamb—is what's for lunch and dinner. And lots of it. The fresh, grass-fed beef of the endless pampas is leaner, gamier, and chewier than the aged, corn-finished American product. For centuries, Argentines have washed it down with rustic, oxidized plonk, but in the past decade there has been an increasing emphasis on quality wines for the export market— the most exciting of which are undoubtedly old-vine Malbecs. The best of these spicy, voluptuous reds are made in small quantities, although they are easier to find in the States than high-quality grass-fed beef. And they harmonize brilliantly with a Black Angus sirloin or a USDA prime rib eye.

Malbec was once widely grown in Bordeaux and is the main ingredient of the big, tannic, rustic wines of Cahors that enjoyed great popularity in Russia during the reign of Peter the Great but have been struggling to find an identity ever since. Sometime in the nineteenth century the grape made its way to Mendoza, roughly six hundred miles west of Buenos Aires, across the sweeping grasslands of the pampas. The province is crisscrossed with an elaborate network of canals, first developed by the Huarpe Indians, which cools the city and irrigates the surrounding vineyards. As they descend toward the plains, the lower slopes of the Andes foothills provide a series of microclimates that can be matched to the ripening characteristics of different grapes.

———

At roughly three thousand feet above sea level in the Mendoza region, Malbec seems to find its ideal home and achieve a complexity and richness that make it a candidate for one of the world's great wine types. Particularly in its youth, Mendoza Malbec tends to be a much friendlier, more cuddly beast than Cahors, and it is almost always rounder, richer, less astringent, and more complete than Cabernet Sauvignon from neighboring Andean vineyards. Not that you'd mistake it for Merlot, which is inevitably less spicy and tannic—a waltz to Malbec's sultry tango.

So much for generalizations. A tasting of top Malbecs and Malbec blends that I attended at Terroir, a by-appointment-only Buenos Aires wine shop, revealed a multitude of styles, not to mention a wide range of quality, which suggests that Argentinean Malbec is a work in progress. The wines that scored highest were boutique wines crafted by transatlantic winemakers: the 2000 Achával Ferrer Finca Altamira Malbec, made from the fruit of eighty-year-old vines by Tuscan winemaker Roberto Cipresso, and the 2000 Yacochuya, crafted by the ubiquitous, genial genius Michel Rolland from similarly antique, high-altitude northern vineyards. The tiny production makes these wines more of an inspiration to their rivals than a regular libation for American drinkers.

Almost as impressive—and widely available here—are the top Malbecs from Catena Zapata and Terrazas de Los Andes, two of Mendoza's largest and most innovative wineries. Catena Zapata, which operates out of a high-tech, Mayan pyramid—think I. M. Pei—winery, introduced the world to the concept of luxury Mendoza Malbec in the early 1990s. Its

2000 Catena Alta Malbec is a worthy successor to previous vintages, a full-bodied, earthy spice box of a wine. The Moët Hennessy–financed Terrazas de Los Andes began production in the mid-1990s, although its top bottling, the stunning, sexy Gran Malbec, comes from seventy-year-old vineyards that have managed to survive the frequent hailstorms plaguing the region. In partnership with Bordeaux's legendary Château Cheval-Blanc, Terrazas also produces a rich, complex, and polished blend of Malbec, Cabernet, and Petit Verdot— Cheval des Andes.

Visiting Mendoza this past spring, bumping into Connecticut wine-store owners and French winemakers in the Park Hyatt, I couldn't help reflecting that the experience must have been a little like visiting the Napa Valley in the '70s, at the dawn of a major international wine scene. Not quite as sexy, perhaps, as watching Carlos Gardel revolutionize the tango in the Abasto Quarter of Buenos Aires in the '20s. But pretty exciting, nonetheless.

PERSONALITY TEST

Julia's Vineyard

I have yet to meet the young lady in question, although by her mother's account she is a beautiful brunette, feisty and high-strung—in the best possible way, naturally—all of which seems appropriate for someone who has a Pinot Noir vineyard named after her. Seventeen-year-old Julia Jackson is the daughter of Barbara Banke and Jess Jackson, of Kendall-Jackson renown. I was fortunate enough to have dinner recently with her mother, her grandmother, and several of the men and women who make wines from the grapes of Julia's Vineyard, one of the oldest in Santa Barbara County and part of the Cambria estate, which was purchased by her parents in 1987.

Located some fifteen miles from the ocean, Julia's Vineyard sits on the Santa Maria Bench, which, along with the Santa Rita Hills to the south, has proved to be the coolest and choicest Pinot Noir real estate in Santa Barbara County. The bulk of the fruit from Julia's Vineyard goes into Cambria's Pinot Noir, making it the answer to the question "Is there such a thing as a good, nationally distributed twenty dollar Pinot?" The Jacksons also sell fruit from these prized old vines to smaller, artisanal producers, including Foxen, Silver, Hartley-Ostini (Hitching Post), and Lane Tanner. Tasting all these wines side by side at the Jackson family's estate just across the road from the vineyard, in the company of the winemakers, provided me with a number of lessons in winemaking, *terroir,* and wine writing, as well as a surfeit of social and sensual stimulation.

Seated to my right was hostess Barbara Banke, the guiding force behind Cambria; she reminds me much more of a first-growth Bordeaux—Château Margaux, specifically—than of a Pinot. A former lawyer who once argued in front of the U.S. Supreme Court, Banke is regal and intellectual, but also extremely warm and approachable (unlike, say, Latour). The Cambria Julia's Vineyard, served with a pumpkin risotto, seemed to me the most delicate and lacy of the 2002 Julia's Pinots, an observation that I have since confirmed in a blind tasting, although I might have been influenced that night by the soft-spoken aspect and gamine appearance of wine-maker Denise Shurtleff, who kept reminding me of a thirty-something Mia Farrow. By comparing Shurtleff to her wine, I realized, I was committing the crudest form of the imitative fallacy that afflicts wine writers: the tendency to equate wine-makers with their wines.

But, hell, my dinner companion Lane Tanner made it all but impossible to resist these easy analogies between wine and winemaker. "My wine is basically the other woman," said the earthy, outspoken forty-something Tanner, whose Web site features a picture of her lying naked in a fermentation tank. "It's definitely not the wife." Although I listened dutifully while Tanner explained that she picks earlier than the other Julia's vintners—this would account for the bright tingle of acidity—her description of her wine as "the perfect mistress, someone you'd pick up in a bar," made a stronger impression than the technical stuff, and I know that when I drink her Pinots in the future, early picking and 23-point Brix sugar levels aren't what I will be thinking about.

The vintners of Foxen (Bill Wathen) and Hitching Post (Gray Hartley and Frank Ostini) were unable to attend the dinner, so my tasting of their wines was untainted by personal impressions. Yet I'm almost embarrassed to say, looking back on my notes, that I found both wines more "masculine" (in the stereotypical sense of the word) and structured than the Cambria and Tanner: a strong note of bacon in the former and a very leathery bouquet to the latter. Tanner, meanwhile, explained that she once lived with Dick Doré, the coproprietor of Foxen Vineyard, who is now married to Jenny Williamson Doré, seated on my right that night, who is Foxen's marketing director and who used to work for Cambria. And Tanner was once the winemaker for the Hitching Post, the restaurant that features so prominently in Alexander Payne's *Sideways*, about which everyone was talking that night. Hitching Post also buys grapes from Julia's Vineyard. Got that?

As I listened to Tanner run through the professional and amorous partnerships and breakups of the Santa Maria and Santa Ynez valleys, my head was spinning. I sympathized with Benjamin Silver, the only male winemaker at the table that night (the Hitching Post boys were in New York for the premiere of *Sideways*), when he said that as a matter of principle he never dated anyone in the close-knit, not to say incestuous, valley wine community. The boyish thirty-three-year-old Silver, who lives in Santa Barbara proper, was clearly something of a pet here among the pioneer winemakers of Santa Maria. His Pinot was the darkest, ripest, and most potent of the evening; whatever happens in his love life, I predict a brilliant future for him as a winemaker.

The next morning, sitting on a hilltop, looking out over the blanket of fog that was gradually receding down the Santa Ynez Valley at about the same rate as the early morning fog in my head, I reflected on the lessons of the previous night. I knew I had discovered a great Pinot Noir terroir. All the wines had impressive structure and balance and shared a certain smoky quality. But the personal signatures of the winemakers were at least as distinctive as those of the soil and climate, which is by no means a bad thing, particularly when the winemakers have such distinctive personalities.

Part Three

HOW TO IMPRESS
YOUR SOMMELIER

HOW TO IMPRESS YOUR SOMMELIER,

PART ONE

German Riesling

Anyone who has been to the movies in the last seventy years knows that the two stereotypes that represent fine-dining anxiety in America are the snotty maître d' and the snotty sommelier (pronounced some-el-yay). Assuming you get past the maître d', the guy with the silver ashtray around his neck is supposed to be a consumer guide, not a bully or a social arbiter. Waiters with a little bit of wine learning can be far more obnoxious than an experienced sommelier. Should you find yourself in a restaurant with an actual sommelier, chances are the wine list is serious. If you're having trouble getting over your fear of sommeliers, here are a few tips on how to make him think you are cool:

If sommeliers have a consistent point of snobbery, it's a slight disdain for or at least weariness with Chardonnay. Tease yours by asking about Austrian Rieslings. All sommeliers love Austrian Rieslings. Then, bring it on home. Ask him to recommend a German Riesling.

Don't roll your eyes. Get over your Blue Nun/Black Tower prejudice. I'd urge you to try German Riesling because it's delicious, but I fear you'll be more impressed if I tell you it's cutting-edge. That, after all, is what we want to know—what's *now* and happening. (Do you *really* think clunky square-toed shoes make your feet look better than those with slimming, tapered toes? You just wear them because that's what fashion dictates, you slut.)

Your sommelier knows that German Riesling in its semidry form currently represents the best white wine value and that it's the most food-friendly wine on the planet. The classic '04 vintage affords a great opportunity to get aquainted with it.

Let's deal with the allegedly vexing problem of sweetness. Many relatively sophisticated drinkers insist that they only like dry white wines. But the fact is that a superripe, low-acid California Chardonnay imparts more sweetness on the palate than many German Rieslings, in which the residual sugar is balanced by a bracing jolt of acidity—which reminds you, if you've ever had the experience, of inhaling a small electric eel. After years of going back and forth, the best German makers have learned to balance these two elements—and while superdry (*trocken*) Riesling continues to attract German winemakers playing against their own strengths, it can be mouth-puckeringly unpleasant.

Get over your fear of residual sugar. A touch of sugar is the perfect complement to most Asian cuisines, especially those dishes with hot pepper. Dry whites turn nasty and bitter in the presence of lemongrass or sweet-and-sour sauce. Given the way we eat now, German Riesling is a far more useful food wine than white Burgundy. (German sweet dessert wines are glorious—but that's another story.)

Concentrate on the *Kabinetts, Spätlesen,* and *Auslesen*—the middle three of the seven official categories of ripeness. *Kabinetts* are light, refreshing, and low in alcohol and range from dry to semidry—I especially like those from the Mosel region. *Spätlese* grapes are picked later; the wines have more body and richness and are often slightly sweeter. Finally, the even riper, richer *Auslesen* can also be drunk with your more robust starters or even your main course. Sweetness varies in these two categories, generally in inverse relation to the alcoholic strength listed on the label. A *Spätlese* with 8 percent alcohol will have more residual sugar than one of 11 percent. But don't worry too much about it. Explore.

One of the reasons wine professionals love Riesling is that no grape (other than Pinot Noir) seems to have a greater ability to communicate the differences between individual vineyard sites. (The French call this *terroir*.) Riesling is the carrier not just of its own grapey DNA but the signature of the soil, subsoil, and even bedrock in which it was raised. Germany's major wine regions present huge variations in geology, providing endless sources of study and tasting debate among well-lubricated professionals. But anyone with taste buds can easily detect, in various combinations, such fruit flavors as lemon, lime, green apple, grapefruit, apricot, and even pineapple in the glass—the latter flavors more likely in the later-harvest *Spätlese* and *Auslese*. But what makes German (as well as Austrian and Alsatian) Riesling profound, like great Chablis, are the permutations of minerality. All have a vibrating, zingy acidity that focuses the other flavors in the wine as well as in your food.

Kabinetts are excellent aperitifs. *Spätlesen* and *Auslesen* go well with a tremendous variety of food: most Asian food, white fish, pork, chicken, and almost anything in a cream-based sauce or cooked with fruit. (The Germans even drink them with beef.)

Nowhere except in Burgundy is the name on the bottle so important. The simplest way to be safe is to look at the back of the bottle for the names of importers Terry Thiese and Rudi Wiest. On the West Coast, Old Vine Imports represents some great growers. Some of my favorites include Christoffel, Schlossgut Diel, Donhoff, Gunderloch, Dr. Loosen, Fritz Haag, Lingenfelder, Müller-Catoir, Selbach-Oster, J. J. Prüm, von Simmern, von Shleinitz, and Robert Weil. Or just ask your sommelier. He'll perk up, as you will when you take that first electric-shock sip.

NO MORE SWEET TALK, OR HOW TO
IMPRESS YOUR SOMMELIER, PART TWO
Austrian Riesling

One of the distinguishing characteristics that set wine professionals apart from the drinking public is a fondness for the Rieslings of Alsace, Germany, and Austria. At tribal gatherings the pros frequently bemoan the resistance of the punters to anything that comes in a tall, thin bottle. "Whenever I notice someone ordering Riesling, I find that I end up talking to him," says John Slover, a sommelier at Cru, chef Shea Gallante's foodie and wine-geek mecca in Greenwich Village. When I dined there with British wine critic Jancis Robinson, I challenged her to pick a heroic white from a wine list that looks longer and thicker than my last novel; she eventually opted for an F. X. Pichler Riesling from Austria's Wachau district. For the past few years, Austrian Rieslings have been the hottest insider's secret in the wine game.

In the preceding chapter I declaimed the glories of German Riesling, but I have found that even those who remain resistant, and sugarphobic, almost always warm to the unique charms of the Austrian juice. Austrian Riesling is generally much drier and more full-bodied than its German counterpart, reflecting warmer weather, while slightly more racy and minerally than the Alsatian stuff. Another way to put it: Austrian Rieslings have great bone structure, but they also have flesh on their bones. The best examples have the precision and mystery of an early Charles Simic poem. *Purity* and *precision* are two words that recur in tasting notes. Think of a samurai sword. Then imagine it simultaneously slicing a lime and a peach. Anyway, I did the other day when I tasted a '99 Hirtzberger.

One prominent critic detects "stones, gravel, and underlying minerals" in a 2000 Nigl Riesling. This splendid redundancy (gravel *is* stone, dude) illustrates the signal feature of great Austrian Riesling: minerality. Tasters like Slover can parse out the traces of granite and gneiss that impart a smoky, tarry taste to a Wachau Riesling, or the limestone and loess underlying vineyards in nearby Kremstal. Any of us can detect the general note of slaty stoniness, which may remind some of drinking directly from a mountain spring.

As far as dry Riesling is concerned, there are three wine regions in eastern Austria that need concern us: the Wachau and the Kremstal, where the best vineyards rise above the Danube River, and the Kamptal, farther north along the river Kamp. Wachau is the most celebrated region for Austrian whites, with vineyards as steep and picturesque as those of Côte-Rôtie and the Mosel-Saar-Ruwer. It's home to the Big Four: F. X. Pichler, Hirtzberger, Prager, and Emmerich Knoll. Close on their heels are Alzinger, Jamek, and Rudi Pichler. Also located here is one of the world's few great wine cooperatives, Freie Weingärtner Wachau, whose excellent wines are a relative bargain.

Wachau has its own classification system of ripeness. The lightest, lowest-alcohol wines are called *Steinfeder. Federspiel* is riper and richer. The highest classification, *Smaragd,* named after a local emerald-green lizard, is roughly equivalent to a German *Spätlese; Smaragds* are full-bodied, rich, and powerful, and can stand up to all manner of spicy dishes and oily fishes.

The Kremstal, to the east of Wachau, also produces some brilliant wines. The soils here are more limestone and clay, as opposed to the gneiss and granite that underlie the hillside vineyards of Wachau. Nigl and Salomon are my favorite producers. The Kamptal region, best known for its Grüner Veltliners, also produces great Rieslings—especially those from Bründlmayer, Hiedler, and Hirsch. Sadly, there is no universally observed classification system that I can discern in these two regions—generally the best wines are named for single vineyards, like the great Zöbinger Heiligenstein, in Kamptal. Alcohol content is a good guide to body and power—not that you will be able to determine this from a wine list. The words *alte reben*— "old vines"—are probably a good sign. And once in a while you will see the German designations of ripeness— *Kabinett, Spätlese, Auslese,* etc.—on a bottle.

The easiest system to follow is to seek out the wines of importers Vin Divino and Terry Theise, the latter a self-described Riesling "wacko" (his company motto is "We spit so you can swallow"). Most of the makers listed above also produce fine Grüner Veltliners, Austria's unique peppery contribution to the wine world. Theise informs me that the Austrians tend to start a meal with Riesling and move on to Grüner. He believes that German Riesling is more compatible with the sweeter dishes of the "modern eclectic multiculti" restaurants. But many new-wave chefs and sommeliers declaim the versatility of the drier Austrian product, and let's face it, some of you will never be converted to the German team.

Austrian Riesling is a natural with the Austrian-influenced food at David Bouley's Danube in New York; it can also get down with many spicier Latin and Asian fusion dishes. "It's the king of wines," says chef Jonathan Waxman, who goes so far as to recommend it with slow-cooked spring lamb. "It can go the distance from white wine food to red wine food." The worst thing I can say about Austrian Riesling is that it doesn't come cheap. A great bottle from F. X. Pichler can cost as much as seventy-five dollars. But you can catch the buzz with examples in the twenty-dollar range from Domäne Wachau or Salomon. The qualitative distance between the good and the great is relatively short. Impress your sommelier or your wine merchant by calling out for a Wachau or a Kamptal Riesling. And prepare to impress yourself.

A few years ago I wrote about the impossibility of finding a wine to compliment asparagus. That was before I went to Alsace and before I had lunch with Olivier Humbrecht and his Scottish born wife, Margaret, in the garden of the Domaine Zind-Humbrecht. Margaret, who looks quite a bit like Téa Leoni, apologized for the simplicity of the lunch, which consisted of just-picked local white asparagus and speck—a light, prosciutto-like ham that is a local delicacy—while Olivier, who is big enough to create his own weather, opened a couple bottles of 1990 Zind-Humbrecht Muscat (which looked, in his massive paws, like half bottles). Apparently, everyone in Alsace knows what I was about to discover—that asparagus and Alsatian Muscat are boon companions. And most wine critics and sommeliers know that Alsatian white wines are more versatile and food-friendly than those of any other wine region in the world, even if they haven't yet convinced the average American wine drinker of this fact.

Alsace has always had a bit of an identity problem, sitting as it does on the border of France and Germany, which have traded it back and forth for centuries. It is in many ways a world unto itself, a north-south ribbon of land studded with medieval villages straight out of Grimm's fairy tales, separated from France by the Vosges Mountains and from Germany by the Rhine River. It the only major wine region in France where wines are labeled by grape varietal—the most important of which are Riesling, Gewürztraminer, Pinot Gris, Pinot Blanc, and Muscat.

Oceans of plonk are produced here for the supermarkets of Europe, but several dozen small domaines turn out complex, site-specific wines that can age for decades. Connoisseurs argue late into the night about the relative merits of Ostertag, Kreydenweiss, Boxler, Beyer, Dirler, Barmès Buecher, Trimbach, Hugel, Marcel Deiss, and Schlumberger. All of these domaines produce great wines. As for me, let's just say I got goose bumps when I turned in the driveway of Zind-Humbrecht, on the outskirts of the little town of Turckheim.

Zind-Humbrecht is a good place to initiate a love affair with Alsatian wines, because it makes virtually every type—thirty-five different cuvées in the '99 vintage—almost half of which is exported to these shores. It's also a showcase for artisinal, natural winemaking; although it doesn't flaunt the fact, Zind-Humbrecht, like several of its neighbors—including pioneers Barmès Buecher and Ostertag—strictly adheres to biodynamic principles of viticulture, a radical form of organic farming. Just in case you like the idea of a chemical-free wine that's been nurtured with the ash of butterfly wings.

Olivier Humbrecht is a twelfth-generation winegrower; in 1947 his father, Léonard Humbrecht, stopped selling grapes to the local cooperative and started buying more vineyards and making his own wines. After a stint in the army and a year in London, where he met his wife, Margaret, at a bus stop on the

Kings Road, Olivier returned to the family business, inheriting more than fifty different vineyards in Alsace. Like an indulgent parent, Olivier sees his job as standing back and letting those plots speak for themselves. I could name six Sonoma Chardonnay makers whose wines taste more similar to one another than do Humbrecht's half dozen cuvées of Riesling, each expressing the soil of its vineyard, fermented by its own local yeasts.

"In twenty years they will make a standardized Chardonnay everywhere," Olivier complained, the only time I saw him scowl in five hours. "In another twenty years there will only be two strains of yeast." Except, presumably, in Alsace. Chardonnay is against the law here. Riesling, which can age for decades, is considered by many to be the most noble variety in Alsace; Alsatian Riesling tends to be a little richer and fatter than its German counterparts. It's also, many of us believe, among the most versatile food wines in the world; though, of course, some pairings are more sublime than others. With his Riesling Herrenweg Turckheim Olivier likes Cantonese food and dim sum; he recommends Gewürztraminer for Vietnamese and Thai food. Essentially unique to Alsace, Gewürztraminer is a rich, heady, and perfumey grape that overwhelms some palates; on the other hand, it can complement powerful flavors like curry and saffron. The third noble grape variety of Alsace is Pinot Gris—which to me often tastes like a smoky cousin of Riesling and which both Olivier and his neighbor André Ostertag recommend as a companion to Peking duck. (Pinot Blanc, a much lighter wine, is better suited to shellfish.)

The three noble varietals are usually fermented till they are relatively dry. However, in certain years good weather allows growers with well-exposed vineyards to leave selected grapes on the vines to produce special Vendange Tardives—late-harvest—wines, which have a higher level of ripeness and sugar. These rich wines fall somewhere between dry and dessert wines. A VT Pinot Gris is excellent with foie gras, less cloying than the average Sauternes, while a VT Gewürztraminer is the perfect companion for Muenster cheese. Every few years the weather suits the production of sublime, extremely late harvest dessert wines called Sélections de Grains Nobles (SGN). These sweet wines will evolve for decades. As for the drier wines—I'm just starting to drink my '99s, although they were perfectly delicious on release. Last night I popped a '96 Trimbach Gewürztraminer Cuvée des Seigneurs de Ribeaupierre, which had a fine dialogue with my Szechuan garlic shrimp.

Don't get me wrong, I have nothing against fruit. But I sometimes get tired of all this superextracted, alcoholic grape juice
that seems like it ought to be served on toast rather than in
a glass, and that tastes like it doesn't come from anywhere
in particular. These are wines that somehow remind me of
the blind date I had recently with a woman exactly half my
age. Our conversation had lots of italics and exclamation
marks and very few parentheses or semicolons. Much as I like
some of the bold new postmodern Riojas from producers like
Artadi, Allende, and Roda, I sometimes crave the sepia tones
of old-school Rioja. Todd Hess, wine director for Sam's
Wine & Spirits in Chicago, is one of many who appreciate
these discreet charms: "Old traditional Rioja tastes like old
Burgundy should taste but seldom does—and for a lot less
money."

What we now think of as the old style in Rioja was created
in the 1850s, when French wine brokers arrived in Spain after
oïdium and, later, phylloxera had devastated their native
vineyards. The French introduced oak-barrel aging to the
region, which had previously specialized in light, fruity, short-
lived plonk. Two nobles, the Marqués de Murrieta and the
Marqués de Riscal, helped develop and market this Bordeaux-

style Rioja. (Both bodegas are still flourishing.) The Riojans took to barrel aging the way the Italians took to noodles, substituting American for French oak and developing an official hierarchy that culminates with *reserva* (at least twelve months in oak, two years in the bottle) and *gran reserva* (at least twenty-four months in oak and three years in the bottle). *Crianzas,* released just two years after vintage, are apt to have a strawberry-vanilla freshness, whereas the *reservas* and *gran reservas* will exhibit the mellow, secondary flavors associated with age—flavors evocative of autumn rather than summer. And those with bottle age can suggest practically the entire spice rack, not to mention the cigar box and the tack room. Somehow you get the idea that this is how red wine used to taste.

If the old school had a central campus, it would be a series of buildings clustered around the railroad tracks at the edge of the medieval town of Haro, including the bodegas Muga and López de Heredia. Both wineries keep several coopers employed year-round, making and repairing barrels and maintaining the huge *tinas*—the swimming-pool-sized oak vats in which the wine is fermented and stored; old oak doesn't impart a woody flavor to wine, and both wineries believe it's superior to stainless steel. Both houses are also run by the direct descendants of their founders. If some evil genie told me I could drink just one producer's Rioja from now on, I would certainly choose Muga. In addition to its old-school wines, notably the *gran reserva,* which spends three years in old American oak barrels, Muga does make a more modern expression of Rioja with French oak under the Torre Muga label, including a new postmodern luxury cuvée called Aro. Not so López de Heredia, the hardest-core reactionaries of Rioja, makers of Viña Tondonia.

Tondonia is one of those secret passwords whereby serious wine wonks recognize their own kind. (Impress your somme-lier, or put him on the defensive, by asking for it.) The winery was founded in 1877, and apparently very little has changed in terms of winemaking since. The Tondonia vineyard is beautifully situated on a high south-facing plateau outside Haro. For reasons not entirely clear to me, the winery com-plex resembles a Swiss or Bavarian village. Inside, it resembles the set of a low-budget horror movie, with ancient and vaguely sinister-looking machinery, huge blackened *tinas,* and a fluffy black mold blanketing almost everything. Some of the vats are as old as the winery itself, and pixieish María José López de Heredia, great-granddaughter of the founder, is convinced that the petrified sediments and natural yeasts in the *tinas* are an important part of the distinct flavor profile of the wines.

Far below the fermentation and storage vats, in a series of tunnels carved out of the limestone, tens of thousands of bot-tles dating from the 1920s slumber beneath the pillowy mold. "The spiders eat the cork flies," López de Heredia explains cheerfully as I swipe a vast cobweb off my face. Any minute now, I feel certain, Vincent Price is going to jump out at me. The sense of eeriness is gradually dispelled, replaced by a mounting sense of exhilaration and wonder as López de Heredia uncorks bottles in the subterranean tasting room. I start with, of all things, a 1995 rosé—this being her idea of a young wine—and move on to the '81 Gran Reserva Blanco, made mostly from the indigenous white grape called Viura, which tastes fresh and lively for its age. The tasting of reds begins with the ethereal '85 Tondonia, which has an amazing nose of cinnamon, clove, leather, tobacco—the whole spice box. While this may sound like one of those annoying instances where you have to listen to a wine writer tease you with descriptions of stuff you will never see or taste, the fact is that all of these wines have been recently released. In this regard, López de Heredia reminds me of Orson Welles's embarrassing ad for Paul Masson: "We sell no wine before its time."

Across the street, Muga is releasing its *gran reservas* on a slightly more accelerated schedule. You can find the '95 and the '96 on retailers' shelves; both have the kind of spicy complexity that develops only with age and both taste kind of like fruitcake, only much better. And if you are lucky, you may find older vintages. A '76 *gran reserva* that I shared with the bearish, gregarious thirty-year-old Juan Muga at a restaurant in Haro lingers in my memory as one of the best old Burgundies I never drank. Marqués de Riscal, Marqués de Murríeta, and Bodegas Montecillo are also good sources of traditional Rioja. Next time you're feeling palate fatigue from trying to chew the latest superextracted New World Merlot, you might consider checking out the subtle and delicate charms of an old *gran reserva*.

THE MYSTERIOUS BEAUTY OF
SAGRANTINO DI MONTEFALCO

If you haven't heard of Sagrantino di Montefalco you're in excellent company. "I've had sommeliers from Italy come into the restaurant who don't know about these wines," says Roberto Paris, the urbane, soft-spoken manager and sommelier of Il Buco, in New York's East Village. Paris had the advantage of being born a few miles from the town of Montefalco, about halfway between Perugia and Spoleto in Umbria. "The very first bottled wine I ever drank was a Sagrantino," he says, wincing at the memory. "It was terrible."

A few years ago, when Paris poured me my first Sagrantino, a '95 Paolo Bea, I had a very different reaction. I felt kind of like Keats encountering Chapman's Homer. Or like I did when I first encountered the work of Umbrian painter Piero della Francesca, which was so singular and weird compared to that of his Roman and Florentine contemporaries. The Bea was a dark beauty in a homemade dress—I was thinking of Michael Corleone/Al Pacino's smoldering, rustic Sicilian bride in *The Godfather*. In an era when Italian wines were starting to taste like Napa wines, this was a wine with soul.

When I went home that night and tried to learn more, my reference library wasn't much help. *The Oxford Companion to*

Wine devoted an uncharacteristically uninformative inch of column space to the Sagrantino grape, noting that Sagrantino di Montefalco received its DOCG status only in the mid-1990s. (It was 1992, actually.) Oz Clarke's *New Wine Atlas* covers Umbria in a single paragraph. Paolo Bea wasn't even listed in *Gamberro Rosso,* the Italian wine bible, although three other makers of the mysterious Sagrantino di Montefalco had entries.

I started looking for Sagrantino on Italian wine lists here in New York and discovered a small, diverse range of wines, most of them fleshy, powerful, bitter, and spicy. Sometimes I was reminded of Syrah, or even Petite Sirah. Sagrantino is fatter, richer, and more tannic than Sangiovese, the dominant grape in neighboring Tuscany. The ideal Sagrantino, to me, tastes like blackberries and bitter chocolate dusted with cinnamon, nutmeg, and clove.

"The origin of the grape is very mysterious," Paris told me recently. "One theory is that the Crusaders brought it back from the Middle East." Presumably, if it were of Roman or Etruscan origin it would have been disseminated more widely. For whatever reason, the cultivation of Sagrantino is limited to a tiny area around the town of Montefalco. Until recently most of the grapes were dried to produce a sweet *passito;* a small fraction was used to make communion wine for the *sacgramenti.* The recorded history of the dry red begins in 1971, when Arnaldo Caprai founded his winery. Caprai is the pioneer who essentially created Sagrantino di Montefalco as we know it—if we know it. The relative obscurity of Montefalco is partly a function of small production; as far as I can tell, there are only ten or twelve serious producers, and most of them are making no more than a couple thousand cases. According to Paris, the other problem—this is Italy, after all—is that "squabbling prevents them from working together."

Caprai is the only producer turning out enough wine to make much of an impact on the marketplace, and the only one who has really taken a scientific approach, experimenting with clones and rootstock. More to the point, the wines are superb and, unlike those of his neighbors, somewhat consistent in character; the funky wines of Paolo Bea, Caprai's rival for the esteem of Sagrantino buffs, can taste very different not only from vintage to vintage but even from bottle to bottle. I imagine him stomping the grapes with his feet and bottling by hand—and I prefer to retain those images rather than calling his importer, Neal Rosenthal, to get the actual facts. In matters of the heart, and of the lower appetites, mystery can often be more stimulating than knowledge.

One thing I can swear to: Bea doesn't use new oak barriques, which is one of the reasons his wines are so je ne sais quoi. Other producers are doing so, and while new oak can round out the rough edges of Sagrantino, it can also, in the wrong hands, make them taste dangerously similar to Tuscan Cabernet or Australian Shiraz. Such is the case with Còlpetrone, which regularly gets the top three-glass award from *Gambero Rosso* (which, scandalously, as of 2005 still has no listing for Bea) and tastes to me like a good Cabernet from, say Stellenbosch, South Africa. Scacciadiavoli switched to new barriques with the '98 vintage without losing too much funky Sagrantino soul.

This is supposed to be the part of the essay where I tell you what a great value these obscure wines are. Sorry. A good Sagrantino costs more than a famous Chianti, if less than a famous Napa Cabernet. The most reasonable Sagrantino right now is Antonelli, not to be confused with the giant Florentine firm of Antinori. But the big firms are getting into the area—recently the Cecchi family from Tuscany bought Tenuta Alzatura, in Montefalco.

Vintage conditions in Montefalco are usually similar to those in nearby Chianti. Some producers are raising prices in the wake of several good vintages and the growing cult status of the wines, not to mention the sickening decline of the dollar relative to the euro. Frankly, I'm ambivalent about helping to spread the word and thereby increase the demand—but, hey, that's my job. Just try not to tell too many of your friends.

Part Four

LOVERS, FIGHTERS,

AND OTHER OBSESSIVES

OEDIPUS AT HERMITAGE

Michel Chapoutier

Michel Chapoutier has a quick answer for one of the thorni-
est food-and-wine-pairing questions ever: what to drink with
asparagus. "The perfect match for asparagus is my competi-
tors' wines," he says. The point is that asparagus tends to make
wine taste metallic and hollow, and this little joke seems to
me to illustrate not only Chapoutier's keen and dry sense
of humor, but also his fierce competitive spirit. Opinionated
and driven, he's an inspiring and controversial figure in the
world of wine. Even his pronounced limp is a manifestation
of his willfulness: he walked around for two months on a broken leg before finally going to the doctor, where an X-ray
revealed four different fractures. But though he needs a cane
to get around now, he seems anything but debilitated; I found
myself at times almost running to keep up with him as he
bounced around the winery and down the sidewalk of Tain
l'Hermitage.

While some writers have invoked Napoleon in describing
the diminutive and fiercely ambitious wine baron, I couldn't
help thinking of Oedipus as Chapoutier described taking
control of the family domaine from his father, "a lazy, violent
man" who belittled his youngest son's capacities and was an
indifferent caretaker of the extensive vineyards he inherited in

the northern Rhône—most notably on the venerable hill of Hermitage, a terroir whose reputation in the nineteenth century was as celebrated as that of Bordeaux. We sat on the porch of his sprawling farmhouse perched on a ridge high above the Rhône, and Chapoutier's anger flared and then faded as he sipped a glass of Trimbach Clos Sainte-Hune Riesling, periodically glancing over at his wife, Corrine, a transplant from Basque country; he met her when he was shopping for an engagement present for his fiancée.

The Chapoutier family arrived in Tain l'Hermitage, in the Rhône Valley, two hundred years ago. They gradually accumulated some five hundred acres of vineyards up and down the valley while establishing a negotiant business in which they bought grapes from other growers and vinified them. The reputation of the house languished under the direction of Michel's father; Michel returned home after oenology school and internships at several California estates to discover the business in a shambles. He took over the winemaking and in 1990, with the help of his American importer, bought the company from his grandfather. (His older brother Marc, who ran the business side, has since been demoted.) Chapoutier consulted with winemakers Gérard Chave in Hermitage and Marcel Guigal in nearby Côte-Rôtie, who introduced the use of new oak barrels in the cellar and lowered yields in the vineyards. Like Guigal, Chapoutier stopped filtering his wines on the principle that it stripped them of character. "Filtering wine," he says, "is like screwing with a condom." (He likes sexual metaphors; when one of his guests struggles to identify the components of a wine's bouquet in the tasting room he urges him to relax and just enjoy the wine. "If you think about it too much you can kill it. The brain is a pleasure killer. You don't need to be a gynecologist to make love.")

Chapoutier went way further than his mentors in his approach to viticulture, virtually banning the use of sprays and chemicals and adopting biodynamics, the radical system of organic farming based on the teachings of Rudolf Steiner. "Biodynamics," Chapoutier explains, "is homeopathy applied to plants." While a number of small producers in Alsace and Burgundy have adopted the system, which is based in part on following lunar cycles, Chapoutier is perhaps the biggest and the most vocal proponent of them all.

Beginning with the strong 1989 vintage, the results of Michel's stewardship were dramatic. In 1996, Robert Parker wrote, "I have never witnessed a more significant jump in quality and change in winemaking philosophy than what has occurred in the Chapoutier cellars since the 1989 vintage." Chapoutier's single-vineyard estate wines (those from his own vineyards, as opposed to those he makes from purchased grapes) are among the most sought-after wines of the Rhône, and the exuberant, hypomanic five-foot-two Michel has become a towering figure in the wine world. Along with his neighbor Gerard Chave, he has helped to reestablish the reputation of Hermitage, a domelike hill best known for its powerful and long-lasting Syrah-based reds, although I find myself most in awe of Chapoutier's white Hermitages, made from Marsanne grapes, wines that are dominated by a striking mineral quality. They don't taste like any other white wines in the world, which to Michel is the whole point of biodynamics—to let the site and the soil speak for itself. "Hermitage was first known for its white wine," Chapoutier says—a claim I haven't been able to corroborate. But no matter. His single-vineyard red and white Hermitages are stunning, powerful, and earthy wines, even better now that he has dialed back a little on his use of new oak. Of his winemaking evolution he says, "I used to be able to make noise, but now I make music."

Chapoutier also makes two superb Côte-Rôties from "the roasted slopes" north of Hermitage, and some of the best wines from the less exalted appellations of Saint-Joseph and Crozes-Hermitage, which are far more affordable than the Hermitages, which can sell for as much as three hundred dollars. And his Châteauneuf-du-Pape, Barbe Rac, made from hundred-year-old Grenache, is usually one of the best. All of these wines are made in fairly small quantities; in recent years he has purchased vineyard land in Aix-en-Provence and in Banyuls, and he now has two different winemaking projects in Australia. "I'm a soil discoverer," he says. He's been called better—and worse. Somehow I don't see him slowing down anytime soon, this whirling dervish who seems driven as much by passion as by his demons.

GHETTO BOYS

Greg Brewer and Steve Clifton Get Radical

The Brewer-Clifton winery is unprepossessing, to say the least—located in an aluminum-sided warehouse in a small industrial park at the edge of Lompoc, California, a town best known for its prison. You definitely didn't see it in *Sideways,* Alexander Payne's movie set in the more picturesque stretches of the Santa Barbara County wine country. Call me perverse, or postmodern, but after all these years of visiting hyper-trophied, gated châteaus in Bordeaux and Napa, I actually find Brewer-Clifton kind of romantic. The warehouse complex also includes ten other wineries and is affectionately known among its denizens as the "wine ghetto." Three decades after Richard Sanford and Michael Benedict proved the area's potential for Burgundian varieties, Steve Clifton, Greg Brewer, and other landless overachievers are working in rented sheds and warehouses to push the limits with radical new stylings of Pinot Noir and Chardonnay.

Before he caught the wine bug, Brewer was a professor of French at the University of California at Santa Barbara; Clifton played guitar in a rock band and was part owner of a nightclub in Laguna Beach. Brewer, who is built like a grey-hound, thanks in part to a fanatic cycling regimen, is the kind of guy who wakes up at three in the morning to check on his daughters and then his vats. Clifton, who looks like a younger version of *CSI* star William Petersen and likes to surf, is liable to be climbing into bed at about that time—or so I imagine on the basis of a couple of nights I spent with him over the past few years, including a chance encounter in Friuli, Italy, that lasted about nine hours. This Apollonian/Dionysian contrast is reflected in the wines, which are almost paradoxical in their juxtaposition of ripeness and acidity, of voluptuousness and bone structure—in other words, wines that speak French but also know how to shake their booty on the dance floor.

When I arrived in the middle of harvest last year, both Brewer and Clifton were hopping between tightly packed tanks and barrels to the rhythm of a loud drum-and-bass beat, courtesy of a CD mixed by Clifton's wife, Crystal, the air thick with the heady funk of fermenting Pinot Noir grapes. Their wine ghetto neighbor Kris Curran, who makes a hot new Pinot called Sea Smoke, stopped by to ask if she could borrow some red wax. (Wax?) Yup, the boys have wax; they use it to hand-seal the corks. Clifton pours me a glass of their Santa Rosa Chardonnay—which starts out deceptively fleshy and round, then zaps me awake with a towel snap of acidity—and explains that the Santa Ynez Valley, with its east-west orientation funneling Pacific air inland, "is a very extreme place; there's some crazy fruit grown here, and you gotta go for it."

Go for it they do—the Brewer-Clifton wines are controversial, and extreme. The duo first met at a Rotary Club tasting in Goleta when they were both working for other wineries. Both dreamed about how they would push the limits if they could make their own wine, and that's just what they've done now that they're on their own. One extreme practice: whole-cluster fermenting for Pinot—i.e., leaving in all the stems, since stems can contribute a green taste, which they believe gives the Pinots additional texture. The Brewer-Clifton grapes come from steep, cool-weather sites, and only a third of the crop is mellowed in new oak before being blended with the rest, which may partly account for the wine's vibrancy.

Clifton drives me east from Lompoc to view some of Brewer-Clifton's sources, the valley getting warmer—as much as a degree warmer per mile, he says. East of the kitschy town of Solvang it's more than warm enough to grow Syrah and even Cabernet, but it's the cool, fog-drenched Santa Rita Hills, between Lompoc and Buellton, that are ideal for the Burgundian varietals. The Chards and Pinots of this region usually have greater natural acidity than their north coast counterparts. None has more zing, more precision and tension, than Brewer-Clifton's. Lovers of fat, buttery Chardonnays and voluptuous Pinots may find them too high-strung.

Clifton points out Ashley's Vineyard, owned by Fess Parker, of Davy Crockett renown, from which Brewer-Clifton purchases Chardonnay and Pinot grapes. On the other side of the highway is the mustard-yellow, Tuscan-style winery of Melville Vineyards, where Brewer is the winemaker and from which the dynamic duo also purchase grapes for their own label. Fortunately, for those who love the Brewer-Clifton style, Melville's Pinots and Chardonnays are made in slightly larger quantities.

As a winemaker, Brewer likes to compare himself to a sushi chef: he's a minimalist who wants to let the grapes and the vineyard express themselves without interference. Whether consciously or unconsciously, the former professor seems to be echoing Flaubert when he says, "I want to be invisible, I want to get out of the way, I don't want a stylistic stamp." The most radical expression of this philosophy is a Melville Chardonnay called Inox, which gets no oak and doesn't undergo malolactic fermentation—the secondary fermentation that creates that familiar buttery taste. Naked Santa Rita Chardonnay, as it were.

"We want to show provenance," Clifton says. The twelve single-vineyard Brewer-Clifton whites and reds "are treated exactly the same, so that what comes through is the vineyard." You'd never mistake their Sweeney Canyon Chardonnay for their Mount Carmel Chardonnay, which comes from a steep hillside dominated by an eerie, unfinished convent overlooking the famous Sanford & Benedict Vineyard. Nor, once you have tasted them a few times, are you likely to mistake Brewer-Clifton's wines for anybody else's.

JILTED LOVER

Auberon Waugh

Novelist Evelyn Waugh, in his fiction and correspondence, provided us with some fine observations on wine and its enjoyment, but perhaps his greatest service to the world of wine was to sire Auberon Waugh. Best known as a novelist, columnist, book reviewer, and curmudgeon, Auberon Waugh wrote a wine column for *Tatler* and later for *Harpers & Queen*. His vinous writing is collected in *Waugh on Wine*, which, page for page, is the liveliest and most pungent wine writing of the century. Waugh called himself "a practitioner of the vituperative arts"; an article he wrote about Islam incited an angry mob to burn down the British council building in Rawalpindi. He believed that wine writing should be no less extravagant and intemperate than political commentary.

"The purpose of the aperitif is definitely not to make one drunk," he says of the first drink of the day. "This should come with the wine, or, failing that, with the port and other delights afterward." This passage displays Waugh's rhetorical powers in all their glory, the first sentence misleading us into imagining that Waugh has gone Methodist or politically correct on us, the second putting that idea to rest with a right jab and a quick left hook. This is called humor, for those of you who have been reading too many wine publications.

"Wine writing should be camped up," he wrote in one essay. "The writer should never like a wine, he should be in love with it; never find a wine disappointing but identify it as a mortal enemy, an attempt to poison him. Bizarre and improbable side tastes should be proclaimed: mushrooms, rotting wood, black treacle, burned pencils, condensed milk, sewage, the smell of French railway stations or ladies' underwear."

He made good on this pledge. "A tremendous amount of unnecessary suffering goes on under the name of liebfrau-milch," he declared. "Filthy" and "disgusting" were his favorite descriptors. As the head of a wine club, he once proclaimed an offering "anal," and was delighted to report that it immediately sold out, a fact that, he felt, said a lot about his countrymen. In a *Tatler* column, he described his cousin's house wine as a drink of "stupendous horror . . . the foul beverage itself tasted of vinegar, blue ink, and curry powder." Not content with this, he said that it reminded him "of a bunch of dead chrysanthemums on the grave of a stillborn West Indian baby," a remark that got him fired from *Tatler*. (He explained to the press council, who called him up on charges of racism, that it was the curry taste that suggested the image.)

Bron, as everyone called him, was more vivid in insult than in praise, but in his wine writing, unlike his literary criticism, he was always looking for love. He described red Bandol as "a beautiful, swarthy, scorched-earth red, which improves with keeping." He could wax rapturous about Condrieu and Châteauneuf-du-Pape. His first love was Burgundy or, rather, a swarthy beverage of that name that he remembered from his father's cellar. He called himself a "jilted lover of red burgundy." In his search for this mythical beverage of bygone country house dinners, he resembled Gatsby in his quest for Daisy Buchanan. Anyone reading Waugh's description of these old Burgundies would imagine he was describing Châteauneuf-du-Papes, and in a sense he was; until the 1930s, Burgundy was regularly beefed up with ripe, two-fisted juice from the Rhône and the Midi. And, naturally, upper-class curmudgeon that he was, he loved port.

Bron's snobbery was tempered by his maniacal thrift—he liked nothing better than a bargain, a cheap Spanish Cabernet or an Italian Merlot that outperformed the great growths of Bordeaux. In fact, what seemed to drive him as an oenophile was the quest for inexpensive substitutes for the wines of Burgundy and Bordeaux. Although he blamed rich Americans for the rising prices of these treasures, and for many of the ills of civilization, he eventually became a fan of Napa Valley Cabernets.

When Bron died in 2001, the vast outpouring of affection in the English press was puzzling to many who had never met him. He had an extraordinarily diverse and devoted army of friends, and they invariably commented on the disparity between his public and private personae. In person his wit was gentle and self-deprecating; he would sooner have drunk liebfraumilch all night than offend a dinner companion. Having once been the target of his satire in print, I was still stinging when I met him at a *Private Eye* luncheon in London a few months later. By the end of lunch I was practically apologizing for having written the book that had elicited his parody.

And I subsequently shared several meals and many bottles

of wine with him. At dinner parties, he was invariably polite, appreciative, and vague about the host's wine. He was far more specific, and pungent, in *Waugh on Wine,* which lovers of the language and the grape should keep at their bedside, to remind us that wine is a subject to inspire passion and polemic.

THE OBSESSIVE

Remírez de Ganuza

In eight years of writing about wine, I've met more than my share of obsessive perfectionists—Angelo Gaja, Helen Turley, and Michel Chapoutier spring immediately to mind. But I've never met anyone more fanatic in his attention to detail than Fernando Remírez de Ganuza of Rioja. Remírez de Ganuza has the shrewd expression of a wheeler-dealer who made his living buying and selling small plots of vineyard land from his neighbors until he finally got hooked and decided to keep the best vineyards for himself and start a winery. He is solidly constructed along the lines of a young Raymond Burr, having the build of a man who possibly enjoys food more than he enjoys exercise—and who sensibly insists that his wines be tasted with food. At the Asador Alameda, in the town of Fuenmayor, he pours five vintages to accompany a multi-course orgy that culminates with the entrecôte of a twenty-four-year-old cow—the owner actually shows us the cow's birth certificate. "Shall we order another one?" Remírez de Ganuza asks me, after we polish off the first platter of meat. *"Sí,"* I say. The rare, charred, geriatric beef is possibly the most flavorful I've ever eaten, and there's more wine to go with it. Each vintage is completely distinct—the ethereal 2000 almost Burgundian, the powerful 2001 more like a Châteauneuf; they show different proportions of a spice rack that includes clove, sage, cinnamon, and balsam.

Everyone I talked to in Rioja told me to visit Remírez de Ganuza despite the fact that he doesn't like anyone else's wines very much. In fact, he insists he has only recently started to like his own wine, the first vintage of which was produced in 1991; he'll admit he likes Latour in a good year, and Vega Sicilia, the venerable property in Ribera del Duero.

Once or twice I've heard other winemakers refer to the fact that the lower third of the grape bunch, the pointy part, sometimes called the foot, is slightly less mature than the upper part, which gets more sun. But until I visited Remírez de Ganuza, I'd never encountered anyone who actually sliced off this bottom tip. In addition to being less ripe, the foot, Remírez de Ganuza explains, is also likely to contain more residual dust and sulfur from the vineyard. After rinsing the foot with the juice on the bottom of the fermentation tank, Remírez de Ganuza sells off this unwanted fruit to the less fastidious winemakers of Rioja. Only the upper "shoulder" goes into his top wine, the *reserva,* which since '98 has been one of the most complex and powerful Riojas. But even before the grapes have arrived at his winery, in Samaniego, they have endured a two-tiered selection process. He harvests the bunches on the southern exposure, those that receive the most sun, first, going back a few days later for the rest.

When it comes time to press his grapes after fermentation is complete, Remírez de Ganuza, who used to be an industrial draftsman, uses a system of his own invention: he inserts a giant rubber bladder in the tank and gradually fills it with water. The grapes are thus pressed gently enough to avoid crushing the bitter pips, and the wine has as little contact as possible with oxygen—which ages grape juice as it does us.

No matter how much care a winemaker takes in the vineyard and the cellar, the fact is that 5 to 7 percent of his bottles will likely be ruined by corks infected with TCA, a cork-loving compound that makes wine taste like moldy cardboard. So not only does Remírez de Ganuza visit the cork producers, but he orders test batches of five hundred corks, each of which he cooks in a small, water-filled glass jar in his lab oven. Any TCA-infected cork betrays its identity by a stench the moment the lid is removed. If more than three of the five hundred corks are tainted, he starts over again, ordering a new batch of corks. Much of this mad science takes place in the beautiful stone cellar beneath Remírez de Ganuza's house in the tiny medieval town of Samaniego. The house appears to be many centuries old, but Remírez de Ganuza designed it himself; it was constructed from stones he bought from an old winery nearby. "Old cellars are too damp," he explains, "and you can't control the humidity." Insofar as it's possible, he's leaving nothing to chance.

This attention to detail is hardly the norm in Rioja, although the 1990s witnessed a revolution in the area, with many new boutique bodegas like Remírez de Ganuza's pushing the Tempranillo grape to new heights of expression. New wineries like Allende, Artadi, Remelluri, and Roda have reinvented the concept of Rioja and have won fans around the world, even as older houses like Muga and Sierra Cantabria have started to produce powerful, fruit-driven Riojas alongside the more traditional and mellower *reservas* and *gran reservas*. The latter, aged in oak for at least two years and in bottle for three more, evoke for me the library of an old house scented with leather volumes and pipe smoke, a style that is faithfully represented by López de Heredia, whose winemaking style hasn't changed since the 1870s, when Rioja rose to prominence after phylloxera devastated the vineyards of Bordeaux.

Remírez de Ganuza has no patience for this mellow old-school stuff. His wines do have some of the same hints of leather and tobacco, along with a medley of spices, but even in a lesser vintage they are packed with fruit—cassis, plums, black cherries, as well as the kind of preserved plums you get in Chinatown. It's as if he both put a massive stereo system in the old library and shelved some copies of García Márquez alongside the Cervantes. Me, I'm happy to live in an era that offers both styles, and that has room for fanatics like Fernando Remírez de Ganuza.

BERKELEY'S FRENCH AMBASSADOR
Kermit Lynch

"Why is it," asks Kermit Lynch, "that most men don't like fat women, but they think they like fat wines?" We're tasting in the cellars of Domaine Tempier in Bandol, near his home in Le Beausset, France, talking about the tendency of the American wine press to celebrate big, superripe wines at the expense of those demonstrating delicacy and finesse. His choice of metaphors reflects the way wine is spoken about in the cellars of Burgundy and the Rhône, though it might not go down so well in liberal Berkeley—where his eponymous wine shop is located, and where he lives half the year.

Lynch is a contrarian of long standing, a California native who doesn't stock a single California wine at his store on San Pablo Avenue, a wine-mad Francophile who thinks Bordeaux has gone to hell, and an admirer of Robert Parker who thinks the man has a fat fetish.

His name alone, encountered on the labels of some of the greatest wines of France, piques curiosity. His appearance is just as distinctive. There is something elfin about the features: the prominent, outthrust ears; the high forehead; the Gothically pointed arches of his eyebrows, which give him a perpetually quizzical, skeptical, leprechaunish mien. His friend Olivier Humbrecht describes him as inscrutable. Lynch claims to be antisocial, though he and his wife, Gail, along with their two children, live a kind of Gerald and Sara Murphy life between Provence and Berkeley, entertaining friends like Boz Scaggs, Alice Waters, and Aubert de Villaine.

As a retailer, importer, and author, Lynch has followed his nose and his palate, discovering and introducing Americans to some of the greatest, most distinctive wines of France. Zind-Humbrecht, Raveneau, Vieux Télégraphe, Mas de Daumas Gassac—these are among his finds. And he has memorably described his quest in *Adventures on the Wine Route,* to my mind one of the best books on wine in the English language, with its uncommon combination of poetic insight and skeptical common sense.

He is a pioneer in his appreciation of the regional traditions of French wine, and his position in the wine world might almost be described as reactionary. Of California wines he says, "I taste them and I wonder, Can a white man sing the blues?" As for the Bordelaises, he thinks they are trying to imitate the Californians. "Bordeaux doesn't taste like Bordeaux," he says over a lunch of grilled vegetables. "It tastes like California Cabernet. The last real Bordeaux vintage was '81. Now they dress their wines up with lipstick and high heels." (Less metaphorically, he thinks the Bordelaises are growing too much, and tarting up the juice with sugar and gimmicks like reverse osmosis, which removes water from the juice.) Describing the old style, he quotes Cardinal Richelieu, who commended the wines of Bordeaux as having "an indescribably sinister, somber bite that is not at all disagreeable." Lynch misses the sinister bite with today's flirty Bordeaux. He gives

Marcel Guigal credit for reviving interest in Côte-Rôtie, while criticizing his heavily oaked blockbusters as lacking regional and varietal character. Opinions like these, not to mention his tendency to corner the market on certain desirable wines, have made Lynch a somewhat controversial figure in the wine world.

By his own description, Lynch was a Berkeley hippie when he first became interested in wine. A musician who wrote for the *Berkeley Barb* and made purses out of Oriental rugs, he found a buyer for his handicrafts business and went to Europe on the proceeds. He returned to California in 1972 and borrowed five thousand dollars to open a tiny wine store. Alice Waters, who had just launched Chez Panisse, was one of his early customers. At the time, the California wine boom was barely in its infancy, and the American market for French wines was largely restricted to the top growths of Bordeaux. Lynch created a niche by visiting the less celebrated regions of France and importing distinctive regional wines. He says his decision to concentrate on European wines was almost accidental; the late California winemaker Joseph Swan was a friend, and Lynch loved his Zinfandels. But when Swan ripped up his best Zinfandel vineyard and planted Pinot Noir, Lynch hated the results. "So rather than lose a friend," he says, "I made a rule: no California wines." One suspects this isn't the whole story, but Lynch gives good anecdote.

In another happy accident, Lynch met the legendary expatriate food writer Richard Olney when looking for a translator on one of his wine-buying trips. (He has since become fluent enough to fend for himself.) Olney's knowledge of French regional wines was as invaluable as his linguistic skills. "He would listen to a wine to see what it had to say," says Lynch. "He changed the way I taste." Like Olney, Lynch believes in context—the context of a wine's origins, and the context of its consumption with certain foods. He scoffs at blind tastings, vintage charts, and numerical wine ratings. "It's ridiculous to rate a Muscadet on the same scale as a Montrachet," he says. "One of the great things about wine is diversity." *Diversity* is his mantra. Yes, he imports Coche-Dury, the hottest white Burgundy on the planet, but he seems just as excited by the inexpensive wines of Corsica, with their unique native grape varietals and herbal aromatics. He recently acquired Les Pallières, an estate in funky Gigondas, in partnership with the Brunier family of Vieux Télégraphe.

Is Kermit Lynch winning his war against homogeneity or losing it? On the one hand, he helped stem the tide in France toward filtration, which he believes—as most authorities now do—strips wines of their character. French regional wines like Sancerre, Chinon, and Bandol have found a place on American wine store shelves. On the other hand, despite local rebellions, the hegemony of oaky Cabernet and Chardonnay advances apace. If you're tired of the same old chocolate and vanilla, you might look for that amazing name on a label the next time you're in a wine store.

THE MAD SCIENTIST OF JADOT

"The tension in the ground—do you feel it?" asks Jacques Lardière, his intense interrogatory gaze almost lifting me off my feet. We are standing in the middle of Clos-de-Malte, a walled amphitheater of a vineyard in Santenay. "You can feel the pulse of the earth," Lardière says, bobbing his head with its wild growth of silver locks while pumping his hands rhythmically in front of his chest. I feel *something* here, looking out at the valley beyond the Romanesque church, basking in the May sunshine and listening to the bees, though it may be the magnetic force of personality of the intensely passionate Lardière, the winemaker for Louis Jadot.

"The minerals," he says, pointing to the ground with one hand and the sky with the other, "must be connected to the light." If only on a metaphorical level, this makes perfect sense. "We are seeking," he says, "the unconscious of the earth." I don't understand all of Lardière's proclamations, but I think he's a better poet than many Bollingen Prize winners, and a genius of a winemaker.

Maison Louis Jadot is one of the oldest and most respected houses in Burgundy, a beacon of consistent quality in a notoriously unreliable region. Jadot is both a domain, producing and bottling wines from its own estates, and a negotiant, vinifying grapes purchased from other growers. Since 1985 the firm has been owned by its American importer, Kobrand, and almost half of the wine, luckily for us, comes here. Burgundy snobs sometimes underrate Jadot's wines because of the firm's relatively large production, but some of us believe that Jadot Burgundies are among the best and longest-lived in the region. And they represent great value at every level, from the humble Beaujolais to the exalted Musigny. If Domaine Romanée-Conti is the Ferrari of Burgundy, Jadot is the Mercedes.

I found it significant that given all the vineyards Lardière could have taken me to, he started in relatively obscure Santenay. "We have to have the same approach for the lesser wines as for the *grand crus,*" he said. And as if to prove his point, later, at lunch in the fifteenth-century Counvent des Jacobins in downtown Beaune, he opened a 1971 Gevrey-Chambertin, a so-called village wine, the third ranking in the Burgundy hierarchy, below *grand* and *premier cru.* Conventional wisdom would suggest that such a relatively modest wine (especially in the half-bottle format he opened) would be over the hill, but this wine was not only still vibrant and fleshy but amazingly nuanced.

What Lardière cherishes—and this is the glory of Burgundy—are the differences between the wines from one piece of ground to the next. As we drive from Santenay north through Chassagne-Montrachet, Puligny-Montrachet, and Meursault, he points out the different vineyards: "That's Combettes . . . that's Charmes . . . *ça c'est* Genevrières." The untrained eye often can't see any logical borders, but a thousand years of empirical observation and tasting have drawn the lines. Later, in the Jadot cellars, Lardière demonstates the indisputable distinctions as we taste the '04s in barrels. There's probably no other cellar in Burgundy where the religion of *terroir* can be so effectively illustrated. Lardière makes over a hundred different wines. The '04 Chassagne-Montrachet tastes much more mellow than the minerally, high-strung Puligny, and the distinctions only become more interesting as we move up the hierarchy. "This is freedom, this is individuality," Lardière shouts, waving his arms and spraying me with some residual Mersualt Charmes. "The grape disappears. It's not Pinot, it's not Chardonnay—it's about expressing the place." (He tries to get out of the way of the process by using the least manipulative techniques.) Considering that he started tasting at seven this morning, his enthusiasm, and the precision of his palate, is impressive.

Lardière can seem alternately—and even at the same time—like a mad scientist and an overstimulated poet; his alter ego at Jadot is Pierre-Henri Gagey, who was preceded in the post by his father, André, and who comes across as the most urbane and polished of French diplomats, although he too is a true believer. "Burgundy is a place of great spirituality," he tells me over a glass of honeyed, minerally '76 Chevalier-Montrachet at his home in Beaune. "Pinot Noir was here in a wild stage when the monks came in the eleventh century. The key of Burgundy is the mutation of Pinot Noir to the environment."

Connoisseurs are pretty unanimous in their praise of Jadot's top whites; in recent years, as I have tasted more and more of the older reds, I've become a devotee. They are darker and slower to blossom than some of their peers because of their long stay in vats and their high fermentation temperature, but they evolve and improve for decades. The '59 Chambertin that Gagey poured with dinner was still brimming with sweet red fruit and hauntingly complex, somehow reminding me of a Valéry sonnet. (Gagey is a bibliophile and we'd been discussing favorite authors.) "It's a very emotional wine," Gagey says—not a bad description. He opened it in part to provide a context for imagining the future development of the 2003 vintage—'59 being a similarly hot and dry year.

The 2003 Jadots were released this past fall—later than most of their neighbors—and I can't recommend them highly enough, especially the reds. The summer was the hottest on record, and while many growers freaked out and picked as early as August 16, when the grapes were technically ripe in terms of sugar content but deficient in flavor development, Lardière and company waited until August 28 and got amazingly ripe and complex flavors. As great as Jadot's 2002s were across the board, some of these will be even better and will be more generous in their youth; yet I already envy the lucky few who will drink the '03 Chambertin Clos-de-Bèze forty or fifty years from now.

VOICE IN THE WILDERNESS

Willy Frank and the Finger Lakes

I usually start yawning when wine people talk about stuff like yeast and sulfur, but Willy Frank gets my attention when he explains, "Sulfur gives wild yeast a headache so they don't go into an orgy."

Like most voices in the wilderness, Willy Frank's is colorful and more than a little strident. "I can prove every word I say" is one of his favorite sentences. His father proved that fine wines can be made in New York State's Finger Lakes region, but the message hasn't really gone wide yet, in spite of periodic encomiums to Dr. Konstantin Frank Vinifera Wine Cellars in the wine press. Nevertheless, the parking lot of the ramshackle winery and tasting-room complex, overlooking riverine Keuka Lake, is jammed with tourists—bikers with antlers mounted on their helmets and parents in matching polo shirts loading up the minivan with cases of wine.

"This region is much better for classic Champagne varieties than Champagne," the highly caffeinated Willy declares within moments of meeting me in the jam-packed tasting room one Saturday afternoon in July. The spry, birdlike seventy-eight-year-old looks like a cheery version of Junior Soprano. "What Champagnes do you like . . . Krug? Bollinger? We can beat them. The grapes never ripen in Champagne." As someone whose parents used to serve Great Western "Champagne," formerly the best-known product of this region, I am skeptical, but Willy never stops talking long enough for me to demur. He reels off a list of gold medals and awards. And the 1997 Chateau Frank Blanc de Blancs he thrusts upon me is a subtle and toasty sparkler, if not necessarily cause for utter despair at the house of Krug. His seriousness in pursuit of sparkling-wine quality is attested to by the permanent blood blisters on his hands, caused by riddling—the *champenoise* process of hand-turning the racked bottles to work the sediment down into the neck. But it is nonbubbly whites, particularly Rieslings, that put Dr. Konstantin Frank Vinifera Wine Cellars—to some extent—on the map.

The Frank family originally hailed from Alsace, migrating to Ukraine some three hundred years ago at the invitation of Catherine the Great, who wished to repopulate the region after a scorched-earth Turkish invasion. Willy's father, Konstantin, a botanist, brought his family to America in 1951 and was drawn to the Finger Lakes region, which was already producing vast quantities of sweet plonk—remember Taylor?—from hybrid French-American grapes.

The area was thought to be too cold for the noble *Vitis vinifera* grape varieties from which the world's great dry wines are made. But Frank realized that the great depth of the glacially carved Finger Lakes moderated temperatures on the hillsides above them, and he eventually planted sixty varieties of *vinifera* above Keuka Lake, making wines that astonished critics and connoisseurs. Nelson Rockefeller regularly sent a plane to pick up cases of late-harvest Riesling, and

Frank's wines triumphed in international competitions. A young Robert Mondavi made the pilgrimage to Hammondsport before starting his own winery in Napa. When Konstantin died, in 1985, his son Willy, a manufacturer's rep based in Manhattan, inherited a run-down and financially precarious estate.

Willy, who often refers to himself in the third person, explains how he turned his father's experimental winery into a commercially viable enterprise: "Willy rips up fifty of the varieties and keeps ten. He replants the vineyards. He busts his chops seven days a week." Switching to first and second person without seeming to pause for breath, he says, "I took a lesson from the theater: I stayed away from New York City till I was ready. You try out in Boston and Philly before you open on Broadway." Frank's wines are now ready for the big time. Le Cirque pours his dry Riesling by the glass, and in 2000 the *New York Times* chose it as best American Riesling—and this is a wine that retails for thirteen bucks.

Frank's other whites are all worth checking out; his barrel-fermented Chardonnay, made from forty-year-old vines planted by his father, could pass for a village Burgundy from Chassagne. And I'm hoping others will follow his lead and plant Rkatsitelli (pronounced ar-kat-si-TELL-lee), a grape from Mount Ararat, which produces a powerful, spicy white suggestive of a dry, more dignified Gewürztraminer. One wine writer has argued that the area's future resides in Gewürztraminer, but Frank points out that aside from being cold-sensitive (and not exactly *hot* in the marketplace), this highly aromatic late-ripening grape is the hands-down favorite of the wild turkeys that outnumber the humans hereabouts. "It's like they have the latest up-to-the-minute cell phones," Willy complains. "They call their friends from miles around to come and eat the Gewürz."

What astonished me on my visit was the quality of the Pinot Noirs, from his fruity twelve-dollar Salmon Run to the herbal and backward forty-dollar reserve, made from forty-year-old vines. I'm going to go out on a limb and say that this region could have a great future with this most temperamental, sublime—and lately fashionable—red grape. (Cabernet seems less suited to the climate—although this year Frank's 2001 Cab won the gold medal at the San Francisco International Wine Competition.)

While a lot of his neighbors are still turning out fermented Kool-Aid from hybrid grapes, the Franks' example is having an effect. Herman Weimer, a German immigrant who arrived in the area in 1968, produces beautiful Rieslings on the western side of Seneca Lake. The deep-pocketed Fox Run Vineyards, also on Seneca Lake, is turning out some good whites and reds—including a fine Pinot—which can only improve as the vines mature. Other up-and-comers: Glenora, Leidenfrost, and Chateau Lafayete Reneau. Dr. Konstantin Frank Vinifera Wine Cellars should continue to flourish under Fred Frank, Willy's son, who may eventually find that he doesn't have to talk quite so fast as his father to convince a skeptical wine world about the virtues of the Finger Lakes.

When they shoved a metal tray with his dinner through a slot in the door of his room, Benjamin Hammerschlag was beginning to think that he'd probably made a big mistake and that he'd be going back to his day job in a Seattle grocery store. He was staying in what passed for a hotel in the Franklin River region of Western Australia, "a pub full of misshapen humanity, pretty much the end of the earth," as he describes it, while seeking out premium wines to import into the States. A week later, with only two prospects in his sights, he woke toward dawn in yet another crummy hotel room, this one in the Barossa Valley, to find the walls literally seething with millipedes. "By this time I was pretty depressed," he says. Fortunately, winemaking in both regions was more advanced than the hospitality industry, and Hammerschlag is a persistent and highly competitive son of a bitch with a very good palate. Over the past five years he has assembled a portfolio, Epicurean Wines, that represents something of a new wave in the Australian invasion.

At the time of his unpromising first visit, Hammerschlag was working as a wine buyer for the QFC supermarket chain in Bellevue, a wealthy suburb of Seattle. In a few years he almost doubled QFC's wine business, deciding in the process that he had a "popular palate." Among the most crowd-pleasing wines he discovered for his clients were old-vine Shirazes from Australia's Barossa Valley, which had just begun to trickle into this country, thanks to a few boutique importers like John Larchet's Australian Premium Wine Collection and Dan Philips's Grateful Palate. "It was a style of wine that Americans loved," Hammerschlag says, "rich and powerful and generous and all about instant gratification." Some Aussies, according to Hammerschlag, refer to these big Barossa Shirazes as "leg spreaders" or, when they are feeling more politically correct, as "T & A" wines. However, given the sheer size and power of these behemoths, stereotypically masculine metaphors seem more appropriate to me; high-octane reds like Kaesler's Old Bastard Shiraz remind me more of a muscle car like a Dodge Charger or a Viper than of a starlet, more of Russell Crowe than Naomi Watts.

The only problem with these South Australian reds, it seemed to Hammerschlag, was that they were pretty hard to find. Potions like Elderton's Command Shiraz or Clarendon Hills' Astralis were made in small quantities from vines, including Shiraz and Grenache, planted in the early twentieth century. (Old vines, it's generally conceded, make more intense and powerful wines than younger ones.)

Although Grange, Penfolds's prototype for premium Australian Shiraz, dates back to 1951, when Penfolds's chief winemaker, Max Schubert, came home from a visit to Bordeaux determined to make a world-class wine, it remained something of a one-off until the 1980s, when others began making big, rich Barossa Shirazes. In just a couple of decades, Australia has become a winemaking superpower, and Australian winemakers circumnavigate the globe spreading their fruity, high-tech gospel.

Much as Hammerschlag loved the big, badass Barossa Shirazes, he was presumptuous enough to believe that there was room for some finesse and more of a specific sense of place in the wines (Grange uses grapes from all over South Australia) and that he could coax even better wines from the country if he could find the right talent. "I consider myself a talent agent," he says. Upon his arrival in Adelaide in '99, he made the rounds of the wine stores and accumulated thirty-six bottles of the local red, which he tasted in his millipede-infested hotel room. Then he started working the phone. He was lucky enough, and early enough, to find a core of extremely talented young winemakers, including Dan Standish, the winemaker at Torbreck; Ben Glaetzer, who was involved with his family's estate; Ben Riggs; and Reid Bosward. In the years since he signed them, Hammerschlag has become more and more involved in the winemaking process, a commitment that has nearly ruined his teeth—the result of tasting through thousands of barrels of tannic young reds.

"I go for that tightrope quality," he says through his dingy choppers one spring evening at the SoHo Grand Hotel, as we slurp the '02 Kaesler Avignon Proprietary Red, which would make a really good Châteauneuf-du-Pape. "Pushing the limits, but still maintaining balance and harmony." To put it another way, Ben's Froot Loops have fiber, and his muscle cars have precise handling and even, sometimes, luxurious interiors. Dan Standish's '01 The Standish, for instance, is the most satisfying young Aussie red I've ever tasted—an old-vine Shiraz that has complex leather and coffee aromatics, an unbelievably voluptuous and viscous texture, and a long, lingering finish that left me alternately giddy and awestruck.

After just two vintages, Ben Glaetzer's Amon-Ra and Mitolo's G.A.M., two old-vine Shirazes, have become instant legends, earning exceptional ratings in the *Wine Advocate,* although like many of Epicurean's wines they are made in tiny quantities. Mitolo also bottles an Amarone-style Cabernet called Serpico that will drive your tasting group into raptures. Fortunately, Hammerschlag has been just as energetic in finding wines for budget-minded hedonists—seriously fun reds like the Black Chook and the aptly named Woop Woop Shiraz. Competitive as he is, Hammerschlag will be furious with me for mentioning that there are some other fine importers, like Appellation Imports, Click Wine Group, Old Bridge Cellars, Old Vines Australia, and Weygandt-Metzler, but nobody is bringing in more consistently thrilling Australian wines than Epicurean.

MOUNTAIN MEN

The Smith Brothers of Smith-Madrone

The temperature plummets as I make the steep ascent of Spring Mountain in my rented Explorer; the redwood forest becomes thicker, damper, and more verdant, threatening to overrun the narrow switchbacks of the road. It's hard to believe I'm just a couple of miles from the arid valley floor and the chic boutiquey hamlet of St. Helena. By the time I reach the top of the Mayacamas Ridge and follow a rutted dirt road down to the Smith–Madrone property, I feel I've traveled back in time to a prelapsarian Napa, a wild paradise with an alley of giant unkempt olive trees and islands of vines—an impression that is only reinforced by the sight of the bearded mountain man on an ancient tractor who looks at me askance, as if I've just beamed down from another planet, and then chugs away without comment.

I'd decided to come here after being knocked sideways by a bottle of the spectacular '97 Smith-Madrone Riesling. I'd never heard of the estate and I was frankly amazed that any American Riesling, let alone one from the warm Napa Valley, could taste this complex—like a great Austrian Riesling from the Wachau. Standing at the top of Spring Mountain in early October freezing my ass off, I felt the Riesling concept (it's a cool-climate grape) beginning to make sense. I'd learned that the estate also made Cabernet and Chardonnay—at prices that hadn't been seen in Napa since the Reagan era. Smith-Madrone is an anachronism in several regards, and I fervently hope it never joins the avant-garde.

Eventually another Grizzly Adams look-alike emerges from the ramshackle barn and introduces himself as Stuart Smith. The taciturn tractor driver, he tells me, is his brother Charlie. "We've been here since '71," Stuart says. "I graduated from Berkeley and came up here. There was a revolution going on. A food-and-wine revolution was starting, too. We wanted to join." What little of his face isn't covered in beard is deeply tanned; and he's wearing a flannel shirt that doesn't appear to have been washed in recent decades. Some of the machinery scattered about the property looks as if it was designed by Rube Goldberg. For a while I imagine that he and his brother have been hiding out here since the Vietnam era, living off the land, a fantasy that is punctured only when he refers to his family in St. Helena, at the base of the mountain. Still, there's no question that the Smith brothers, who arrived just a few years after Mondavi set up shop on the valley floor, are pioneers, and that they have a very distinctive *terroir*.

"There is no actual Spring Mountain," Matt Kramer tells us in his *New California Wine*. "Instead it's a colloquial term used in Napa Valley to refer to a section of the Mayacamas range at the midpoint of the valley just west and north of St. Helena. The name derives from the numerous springs and creeks on the mountainside." Stuart says that vines were first planted here in the 1880s—they found old wooden stakes among the redwoods and the madrone trees. California's first great Chardonnay estate, Stony Hill, was established here in the 1950s, just below the property that is now Smith-Madrone. Nearby Pride, a relative newcomer to the ridgetop, is producing massive, high-scoring Cabs and Merlots. Meanwhile, the Smith brothers have built a loyal following with distinctive, modestly priced reds and whites without attracting a whole lot of wine media attention.

If Riesling were more fashionable, this estate would be famous. Smith-Madrone's comes from a six-acre dry-farmed vineyard. ("If you irrigate the vines they don't ripen as nature intended," Stuart says.) While it is delicious on release, bursting with green apple and peach flavors, it develops tremendous depth and complexity with age. The '97 is still youthful, stony and vibrant, while the '93, which Stuart opened for me with his Swiss Army knife after rummaging around the ramshackle barn that serves as a winery, tastes like deep-dish apple pie with an enlivening splash of lemon juice, a dusting of sugar, and an underlying minerality. "Riesling's for aging," Stuart says, "and Chardonnay for drinking." Smith-Madrone makes a fine Chardonnay as well; it has more fruit up front but is better balanced with acidity than most Napa Chardonnays.

Spring Mountain is best known for its Cabernet, and Smith-Madrone's are fine examples, with the area's massive depth and tannin along with a hint of dill, the signature of the American oak barrels. Stuart says they started with American oak barrels for reasons of economy, French oak being much more expensive. I point out that fans of Silver Oak Cabernet happily pay sixty to a hundred bucks a bottle for the taste of American oak. Stuart shakes his head censoriously, dislodging a few drops of the Cabernet from the mustache covering his upper lip. "We think thirty-five bucks is a lot to pay for a bottle of wine," he says. "Maybe we're crazy. People were stopping my son Sam on the street in St. Helena and saying, 'You've got to charge more for your wines.' But then, after 9/11, when everyone was having trouble selling wine, we had our best year."

When I woke up the next morning in my hotel room in Yountville I actually wondered if I had dreamed the whole Smith-Madrone experience—the grizzly brothers, the wild mountaintop, the hypertrophied olive trees, the unreal prices, the anamolous and ambrosial Riesling. I have since confirmed that it was all real and wrestled with the question of whether or not to share this information with my readers. I advise you to get on their mailing list before the Smith brothers realize it's the twenty-first century.

DO THE BRITS TASTE DIFFERENTLY?

Michael Broadbent and Jancis Robinson

So far as I know, none of the online wine chat rooms has ever hosted a spirited debate about whether Michael Broadbent is a babe. That's just one of the ways in which he differs from his fellow Master of Wine Jancis Robinson, although they are both extremely snappy dressers: Broadbent favors Savile Row tailoring, while Robinson is a devotee of Issey Miyake. If there is an English, as opposed to an American, palate, these are its two avatars, representing the traditional and the new wave of British wine writing, respectively.

Now that the second great American Revolution—the one in which Robert Parker played George Washington—has become the new wine orthodoxy, it can be curiously refreshing to check in on the old country. At New York's Veritas, a holy site for American wine drinkers, Broadbent's entrance causes a stir. Even those diners who don't recognize him pause to take in the tall, stately figure who somewhat resembles the late Ralph Richardson, with the addition of a full head of silver hair. After a few minutes, Broadbent pierces the churchly hush with a loud declaration. "You Americans bloody well should drink more," he says. "There's too much talking and writing and sniffing and tasting. Drink!"

As, since 1966, the head and later the executive director of

Christie's wine department in London, Broadbent has tasted more old bottles than almost anyone on earth, and has kept notes on all of them—137 identical red notebooks full of scrawled commentary, transcribed by his wife, Daphne. His *Vintage Wine* is an incomparable record of fifty years of tasting that covers some three centuries. At one point in the evening we found ourselves discussing the '67 Yquem. I thought we were talking about the 1967, whereas Broadbent was referring to the 1867.

Broadbent is one of the last representatives of a great tradition of Bordeaux-centric British oenophiles. Above all else he loves the slightly austere, Cabernet-based wines of the Médoc, which have been the backbone of the English wine trade for centuries. His was a generation, as Jancis Robinson told me recently, "who thought even Pomerol slightly vulgar." When I ask him about this he concurs, saying that the wines of Pomerol and Saint-Émilion "are too easy. Even Pétrus, it's a little like Gewürztraminer: after a few sips, I'm tired." This sounds shocking in 2004. For the past two decades the small-production, Merlot-based wines of the right bank, like Pétrus and Le Pin, have become more fashionable and expensive than Latour and Lafite. He is similarly skeptical about many of the "garage wines" of Saint-Émilion and the cult Cabernets of California, although he is open-minded enough to judge them individually. (He loves Screaming Eagle.) Here's his note on the '97 vintage of the superfashionable Le Tertre Roteboeuf: "One of those modern, chocolaty, very sweet, very fleshy, over-the-top wines. Frankly awful." (I agree with the first sentence and disagree with the second.)

Although a Robert Parker blurb graces the back of *Vintage Wine,* and Broadbent says of Parker, "I admire his honesty and thoroughness," Broadbent is, for all intents and purposes, the anti-Parker. At Veritas he tells me, "Parker doesn't understand the difference between fruit and wine." Most of the wine that Broadbent admires has long since lost its youthful fruit. The new international style of wine, he claims, tastes like the product of "two machines, one with black currant and one with vanilla."

Jancis Robinson was the first wine professional I ever met—at the table of novelist Julian Barnes some fifteen years ago. Although I found her dauntingly attractive, I was relieved that she was modest and unpedantic; in the end we almost had to beg her for some comments on the wine. Besides being entertaining, her remarks somehow made me feel smarter. That evening helped demystify wine appreciation for me. I suspect Robinson has done the same for many readers over the years. Robinson passed the grueling Master of Wine exam in 1984, back when the MW was largely a badge of the hypermasculine Brit wine trade. In the past two decades she has become a major star in the dowdy world of wine. The wine columnist for the *Financial Times,* she is best known to American oenophiles as the editor of *The Oxford Companion to Wine* and for her former column in the *Wine Spectator.*

The glamorous, scholarly Robinson has helped shape a more wide-ranging, global thirst in Britain; it might be said that she has an international palate. (Which is not to say that she can't identify a '61 Cheval-Blanc blind, as I once watched her do, although she is the first to admit that her husband, restaurateur and food writer Nick Lander, is the champion blind taster in the family.) She was one of the first non-Aussies to take Australian wines seriously, making her initial visit there in 1981. She was also an early champion of the Languedoc, and she recently traveled to China to explore the vineyards there.

She believes that the new wave of British wine enthusiasts is more adventurous than its American counterpart: "The Brits fall all over themselves to view the vinously newfangled in a favorable light. Ecuadoran Viognier, yes please! Just so long as it doesn't cost more than £4.99." Americans can keep abreast of these kinds of insights through her excellent Web site, jancisrobinson.com. On the other hand, if you should ever find yourself considering the purchase of, say, an 1899 Lafite and wondering how it compares with the 1898 or the 1900, or if you just want to indulge in some literate wishful thinking along these lines, her friend and colleague Michael Broadbent is your man.

ROBERT MONDAVI'S BIZARRO TWIN

The Passions and Puns of Randall Grahm

Randall Grahm's plans for world domination have suffered numerous setbacks at the hands of litigious wine barons, the hegemonic California Cab/Chard axis, and glassy-winged sharpshooters, but he doesn't seem remotely discouraged. At forty-nine, he has the youthful appearance of an underfed grad student, ponytailed late-1960s University of California at Santa Cruz edition, and exudes an enthusiasm only slightly tempered by wry wit and skeptical intelligence. When we met for lunch recently at the Union Square Cafe in New York, he was greeted like a rock star, not only by the staff but by fellow diners, who repeatedly interrupted us to kiss his ring. (Not that it bothered me. Really. Even though New York is supposed to be *my* turf. I was totally fine with that.)

Grahm is one of the eccentric visionaries of the wine world, in the same unclubbable club as Didier Dagueneau, Sean Thackrey, and Stanko Radikon. He is the founder and proprietor of Bonny Doon Vineyards, godfather of California's Rhône Rangers, the Bizarro Universe's evil twin of Robert Mondavi. Readers of his newsletter may suspect that Grahm got into the wine business in order to indulge his literary bent, marked by a taste for outrageous puns ("carneros knowledge," "mail freud," "entre noose") and abstruse references to literature, philosophy, and Chinese medicine. A recent issue includes a Salinger parody entitled "A Perfect Day for Barberafish." Grahm also penned a parody of *The Bridges of Madison County* back in the heyday of that tearjerker, with übercritic Robert Parker cast as the romantic lead.

Grahm's wine jones kicked in when he was studying philosophy at USC and took a job at a wine store in Beverly Hills. "It seemed like a good way to meet girls," he says. At the store, Grahm tasted some of the great French wines. "I realized that the only way I was ever going to be able to afford wines like those was to make them myself," he says. Pinot Noir was his first love, but he discovered the wines of the Rhône Valley through his friend Kermit Lynch. Grahm decided that Rhône grape varietals were better suited to California, and the rest is wine-geek history. He wasn't the first California Rhônephile—he credits David Bruce—but he was probably the Elvis Presley of the so-called Rhône Rangers.

While Napa was becoming famous for its Cabernets and Chardonnays, Grahm sought out old vineyards of Grenache and Mourvèdre, and planted his own grapes near Santa Cruz. Among his first successes were two New World versions of Châteauneuf-du-Pape that, besides impressing the critics, demonstrated his talent for outrageously clever names. His Old Telegram is an homage to Vieux Télégraphe; Le Cigare Volant is a reference to an ordinance passed by the town council of Châteauneuf-du-Pape banning alien spacecraft, known in France as flying cigars, from landing within the town limits. Grahm's dessert wines, particularly his sweet Muscat, have received outstanding scores from Robert Parker.

Grahm's airship of a career seemed to lose altitude in the '90s. His vineyards were among the first to be wiped out by Pierce's disease, spread by a nasty insect called the glassy-winged sharpshooter. (I was clever enough to purchase the last vintage, a case of his 1994 Bonny Doon Syrah, one of the best New World Syrahs I've tasted.) Parker stopped reviewing Grahm's wines for many years—either through lack of interest or because of the *Bridges of Madison County* parody. The movement Grahm had begun made it harder for him to purchase grapes.

On the other hand, he started Ca' del Solo, a line of Cal-Ital wines made from Nebbiolo, Barbera, and Pinot Grigio. He planted more than eighty acres of grapes in Soledad, illuminated at night by the prison's spotlights. And he was the first American winemaker to experiment with microoxygenization, a method of oxygenating wine to soften its tannins and (theoretically) extend its life.

The most innovative move for this inveterate innovator was the creation of his wine club—called DEWN (get it?), for Distinctive Esoteric Wine Network—a new paradigm for marketing wine and a new winemaking concept of one-off creations. The DEWN wines are single-performance tours de force, sometimes made in collaboration with European winemakers. To create his '99 Fish out of Water Ripasso, Grahm passed Nebbiolo juice over raisiny dried Barbera skins. "Why?" he asks. "Because we could." The massive, black curranty 2000 Le Monstre was made in the Languedoc in collaboration with a French winemaker, while the voluptuous '99 My Favorite Marsanne nearly earned its title for this taster. The good news is that anyone can join the club, and the wines are ridiculously reasonably priced. The weird news is that they are made only once—wine as performance art. "Traditionally, winemaking is about tradition and continuity," Grahm acknowledges. But he seems to believe that life is too short to exhaust all of his winemaking concepts, not to mention his store of wacky names. The labels, by artists such as Ralph Steadman, are just as—how you say?—inventive. As a philosophy major—and a Riesling lover—I can't resist a wine called Critique of Pure Riesling. But Grahm's wit has cost him points in snottier corners of the wine world. Show-offs don't break out a wine called Macho Nacho for client dinners.

For all of his iconoclasm, Grahm is ultimately a wine conservative. He rails against the overuse of new oak barrels and oenological "Viagrafication." "Both Parker and the *Wine Spectator* have oversimplified wine," he says. "It's all about intensity and power. Valuing a wine for intensity is like judging music on how loud it is. Strangely," says the posthippie, who regularly gets his chi adjusted, "I'm kind of a Tory about wine."

Kind of.

Part Five

EXPENSIVE DATES

FIRST AMONG FIRSTS?

The Glories of Cheval-Blanc

Platonic absolutism ultimately seems foolish in the ecstatic realm of Bacchus. There's an ineradicable, subjective component to the appreciation of wine. That said, no wines in the world command quite the respect of Bordeaux's Big Eight. And, speaking strictly subjectively, I can say that no wine has given me more pleasure than Cheval-Blanc.

Lafite, Latour, Margaux, and Haut-Brion were the original first growths in the 1855 classification of Bordeaux; by the time Mouton-Rothschild was added to the list, more than a hundred years later, three other properties—Pétrus, Ausone, and Cheval-Blanc—enjoyed unofficial first-growth status. These three mavericks came from the right bank of the Gironde River—from the communes of Pomerol and Saint-Émilion. Before the Second World War, the right bank was essentially Burbank to the left bank's Beverly Hills, Brooklyn to the Médoc's Manhattan.

Although Cheval-Blanc steadily gained recognition after its purchase by the Fourcaud-Laussac family in the mid-nineteenth century, the real fame of the château was established with the 1947 vintage—probably the most coveted wine of the century. Despite a string of brilliant incarnations since,

Cheval was somewhat overshadowed by neighboring Pétrus, which became the most expensive wine of Bordeaux, and by the left bank aristocrats who, through the '80s and early '90s, duked it out for 100-point Parker scores. In the mid-'90s, Saint-Émilion—like Brooklyn—became fashionable, thanks in part to ambitious winemaking, clement weather, and the accessibility of its Merlot-based wines. In 1998—one of the greatest right bank vintages of recent years—Cheval-Blanc was purchased by luxury-mad Bernard Arnault, of LVMH, and Baron Albert Frère, a Belgian tycoon. As of 2006, no wine property is hotter than Saint-Émilion's premier château, although Cheval-Blanc is in some ways a republic unto itself, resembling no other wine in the world.

Located on the border of Saint-Émilion and Pomerol, Cheval-Blanc has qualities of both—and of neither. Its combination of earthiness and sophistication reminds me (note earlier comment re subjectivity) of Turgenev, who had one foot in Russia and one on the Continent—and who has probably never been a *Jeopardy!* answer, like Tolstoy (Lafite? Pétrus?) or Dostoyevsky (Mouton-Rothschild?). The pretty, modest nineteenth-century manor house and the modern winery next door probably won't show up on the cover of a design magazine. The real beauty is underground: the estate encompasses three different soil types; 40 percent of its subsoil is the same clay that pops up a few hundred yards away at Pétrus. But Cheval-Blanc is unique among the wines of Bordeaux in part because of its high percentage of Cabernet Franc—usually more than 50 percent of the blend. The wines of the left bank are predominantly from Cabernet

Sauvignon; those of Pomerol and Saint-Émilion are mostly Merlot.

Unlike the other big Bordeaux, which take half a lifetime to get sexy, Cheval-Blanc is approachable and even delicious in its youth, and yet it continues to develop over the decades. Imagine a child star who remains a top box-office draw into her sixties. I can't explain the chemistry, but I know from experience that the tannins in the typical Cheval-Blanc are like cashmere compared with the scratchy Harris tweed tannins of Latour or Mouton-Rothschild (and even Pétrus), which take twenty years or so to mellow and drape correctly. Which is not to say you should guzzle Cheval soon after it is bottled. The aromatic complexity of a forty-year-old Cheval-Blanc in a great vintage such as '64 or '55 is like a catalog of minor vices: tobacco, menthol, coffee, truffles, and chocolate, to name a few.

Many tasters claim that the '49 is at least as great as the '47—a freakish hot-vintage wine that stopped fermenting before all the sugar was converted to alcohol, leaving some three parts per thousand residual sugar, which makes it resemble nothing so much as a great port. It was clearly a one-off, a spectacular wine that lingers on the palate for minutes and in the mind forever. Generally, Cheval-Blanc is more lyric than epic, more Andrew Marvell than Milton. I love the '55, my birth year. The '61, gorgeous as it is, is not as profound as the '64, one of my top three wines of all time; I have tasted it several times, thanks to Julian Barnes, who loves it beyond all other Bordeaux and has a stash in his cellar.

The '75 is one of the few wines of that vintage that has lived up to expectations. Parker gives 100 points to the '82 Cheval, but I find it less rich and concentrated than the '83, the '89, or the '90. (The latter appears to be evolving very rapidly, in my recent tasting experience, seeming far more mature than most vintages of the '80s.) Pierre Lurton, the dynamic young director of the estate and scion of a famous Bordelais family, told me at a recent tasting at New York's Veritas that he too feels the '82 may be slightly less than perfect. Nineteen eighty, he points out, was a monstrously prolific vintage, and it was the last one at Cheval-Blanc in which no green harvest or barrel selection was made. Since then the château has lowered its yields in the vineyard and been more selective in the cellar.

After years of being a connoisseur's wine, Cheval seized the spotlight with the 1998 and 2000 vintage. There have been, alongside the kudos, grumblings that the new regime is determined to become the Pétrus of Saint-Émilion, in terms of price as well as quality. Thanks to Parker and others, the 1998 was a legend almost before it had been pressed, and the 2000 looks like the star of that great vintage. "You can't make the price stick if nobody wants to buy it," says Todd Hess, wine director of Sam's in Chicago, who can't satisfy the demand from customers who want to pay six thousand dollars for a case of the 2000 vintage.

Unfortunately for those of us who have to ask about the price of things, the days of Cheval-Blanc as the sleeper star of Bordeaux are over. But for those who aren't hung up on famous vintages, the '99 is a great claret and a great Cheval for less than half the price of its famous siblings, and the 2001 appears to be another sleeping beauty. Other great vintages can be purchased at auction for far less than the cost of the 2000. Any Cheval-Blanc that you can afford will reward your investment lavishly, and its pleasures will probably outlast your capacity to enjoy them.

THE NAME'S BOND

Harlan Estate was the first of the cult Cabernets that swept into the Napa Valley in the nineties like guerrillas coming down from the hills, challenging the preeminence of such valley-floor aristocrats as Mondavi and Heitz. Less than two decades later it's a classic, the most consistently celebrated and coveted Napa Cab of them all. Meanwhile, owner Bill Harlan and winemaker Bob Levy have been creating a new wine—or, rather, three new wines—along with what may be a new paradigm or, at the very least, a new name to make connoisseurs and collectors salivate. The name is Bond.

The Harlan team recently released three Bond wines from the great 2001 vintage under the names St. Eden, Melbury, and Vecina. Having tasted them at the winery, I can vouch for the fact that they are all Harlanesque—an adjective Robert Parker defines as "meaning first-growth Bordeaux complexity combined with Napa ripeness and power"—but they are also noticeably different from Harlan and from one another. They are basically single-vineyard wines from special hillside sites around Napa, a fact that reflects the trend of increasing site specificity as you travel up the price-and-prestige scale (a wine labeled "Oakville" being presumably more singular than one that lists California as its provenance). When I say "basically"—well, hold that thought.

Ever since he'd started visiting the great vineyards of France as a wine loving real estate developer, Harlan had dreamed of creating a California "first growth—a property to rival the great domaines of Bordeaux." Before he created Harlan Estate, stitching together prime hillside parcels over-looking the famed Martha's Vineyard, Harlan founded Merry-vale Vineyards in 1983. He conceived Merryvale as a learning experience. Harlan and his partners bought grapes from more than sixty different growers in Napa, discovering what they considered some extraordinary grape real estate. "Bob Levy said to me, 'You know, some of these vineyards are first growths,'" Harlan says. "But I put that behind me for a while." Not for long, though.

While some critics wondered if Harlan Estate and similarly ultrarich, small-production boutique Cabs that emerged in the nineties were flashes in the pan, Bill Harlan was thinking about the future. "For Harlan to last for generations we had to make sure we didn't become too insular," he says. "And we had to groom the next generation. Harlan Estate was too small for that." Harlan had no desire to expand the produc-tion (about fifteen hundred cases) of his estate wine at the risk of compromising quality. But he and Levy hadn't forgotten about some of those great vineyard sites from their Merryvale days, and they began talking to the owners.

The Bond concept, which Harlan began to develop more than a decade ago, was of "a stable of Thoroughbreds." The stable would be run by the Harlan team, including Bob Levy and superstar consultant and *Mondovino* star Michel Rolland, but it would be entirely separate from Harlan Estate. It would be a brand with individual stars.

The challenge they faced was that it's very difficult to create great wine using other people's grapes, since the buyer's and seller's motives are basically at odds. Growers, especially if they are paid by the ton, want to maximize their yields to maximize their profit, and high yields are the enemy of concentrated wine. The solution, as many grape buyers have concluded, is to pay by the acre and not by the ton, encouraging the growers to strictly limit yields. In creating Bond, Harlan seems to have gone a step further than usual by devising a long-term profit-sharing plan with his growers.

The name Bond, besides being a family name on his mother's side, is intended to convey this idea of a mutual partnership between the Harlan team and the various growers. Harlan speaks of it as "a convenant." If this sounds a little fervent, all I can say is that great wines are inevitably the result of an obsessive vision. And Harlan has figured out a way to keep these vows intact. "It takes ten to twenty years," Harlan says, "to build a name, for us to make these vineyards recognized." Under his agreement with the owners, the vineyard names under which Bond produces the wines can only be used jointly. If a grower and Bond later part ways, neither can use the name again. Even more unusual is that Harlan reserves the right to tinker with the blending of the Bond wines if vintage conditions call for it, in order to maintain a Bond standard. Thus the possibility exists that a future Bond Melbury may be fine-tuned with juice from Bond or Harlan vineyards—a fairly radical concept, since it mixes the seemingly contradictory single-vineyard ideal with the idea of a proprietary house style, making for a kind of a virtual single-vineyard wine. "It hasn't happened yet, but we're allowing ourselves the option to make a better wine," Harlan says, and hence there is no actual geographical information on the label. Wine purists may balk at this concept. But Harlan believes that "the discerning wine consumer of the twenty-first century wants a consistency of quality." And he should probably expect it at a hundred and fifty a bottle.

Bond started with two vineyards, Vecina and Melbury, about eight acres each, and added a third, St. Eden, with the 2001 vintage. (The eventual goal is six Bond wines.) Based on the '01 and '02 vintages, the only ones I've tasted, the Vecina is the powerful, structured, action-film vineyard, the Latour of the group, while the Melbury (my favorite) is more lush and delicate, like a great Pomerol; the St. Eden (which has garnered the highest Parker rating) seems to split the difference. The '03 wines may be even sexier than the '02s and are eminently worthy of their illustrious pedigree. Just when I think I'm bored by Napa Cabernets, along comes Bond and its stable of Thoroughbreds. After tasting the wines, I'm thinking that rules are best left to the French.

"A GOOD AND MOST PERTICULAR TASTE"

Haut-Brion

Haut-Brion saved my life. Well, maybe not my life, exactly, but certainly my dignity. I'd arrived late for a dinner at La Grenouille, the stuffy New York temple of haute cuisine. Eleven other guests were seated; the hostess, an Asian princess, announced, "Here's Jay—he knows wine. He'll guess what we're drinking." Before I could find a heavy object with which to bludgeon her, the sommelier handed me a glass and poured from a carafe. He stood back and smirked, while the other guests looked up at me expectantly, as did diners at nearby tables.

The whole setup reminded me of the dream in which I stand naked in front of a classroom. With a sense of resignation bordering on despair I stuck my nose in the glass. "Haut-Brion," I declared, eliciting a chorus of gasps. I examined the color, and took a sip. "Nineteen eighty-two," I pronounced.

I sat down and basked in the general admiration without bothering to explain my methods—but now the secret can finally be revealed. I knew my hostess generally drank first-growth Bordeaux and I knew she knew her vintages. But I was very lucky that the wine was Haut-Brion—the most aromatically distinctive and unmistakable of all the first growths; as the great English diarist and bad speller Samuel Pepys put it, in the first brand-name reference to a wine in English literature, "Ho-Bryan . . . hath a good and most perticular taste that I never met with before." To be more specific, a mature Haut-Brion smells like a cigar box containing a Montecristo, a black truffle, and a hot brick, sitting on top of an old saddle. It's as earthy and complex as a Shakespearean sonnet. Once you've had it you never forget it, and you never stop yearning for more.

In the seventeenth century owner Araud III de Pontac created the first Bordeaux brand, refining winemaking techniques and sending his son to London to tout the product; Daniel Defoe, Jonathan Swift, and Thomas Jefferson were among its early, vocal fans. Contemporary advocates include the Wachowski brothers—the 1959 Haut-Brion makes a cameo appearance in *The Matrix Reloaded*.

In 1855 Haut-Brion was officially listed as one of the four first growths of Bordeaux. In 1935, after a long period of decline, the property was purchased by American banker Clarence Dillon and has remained in the Dillon family ever since.

When I had lunch at the restored sixteenth-century château this past spring with Clarence's granddaughter, Joan, the Duchess of Mouchy, I asked about the legend that Dillon had not even bothered to get off the train in Bordeaux in order to see the property before he purchased it. "That's absurd," she said. "He looked at several properties, including Haut-Brion. He was in the middle of the Atlantic on his way home when he got a telegram from his agent saying that Haut-Brion was still available but he would have to act fast. He sent a two-word reply: ACT FAST."

Dillon, who spent some of her formative years in Paris

when her father was the American ambassador and was formerly married to the Prince of Luxembourg, has a voice evocative of a privileged transatlantic upbringing, as deep and burnished as an old Vuitton steamer trunk. She also has a cache of anecdotes that would have made Truman Capote wild with jealousy—unfortunately, she's probably far too well brought up to write a memoir. Since 1975 she has run the estate with the aid of Jean Delmas, the most respected winemaker in Bordeaux, who inherited the *régisseur* duties from *his* father, George, and claims to have been born "in a vat" on the estate.

The continuity of the Haut-Brion tradition is clearly a sacred duty to the stately, impeccably tailored Delmas, whose son Jean-Philippe seems poised to succeed him, though, like Arnaud de Pontac, he has pioneered many innovations, being among the first to employ stainless-steel fermentation tanks and green harvesting—the pruning of excess grape bunches to ensure concentration. He maintains an experimental garden of some 350 vine clones out behind the château; they are vinified and tested, and the results charted by computer. He tried to explain the process to me, but I got dizzy just looking at the charts.

For centuries, connoisseurs like John Locke, Jefferson, and McInerney have made the pilgrimage to this holy ground in the Graves region, just south of the city of Bordeaux, to examine the sandy glacial soils, full of gravel, which range in color from ash white to espresso brown; today, the vineyards are hemmed in on all sides by the dreary suburban sprawl of the town of Pessac. But the wine retains its subtle, inimitable, lonely majesty.

Haut-Brion's elegant, supple house style is, in my opinion, often undervalued by wine critics, vis-à-vis the more masculine wines of the Médoc (and its former rival and next-door neighbor La Mission–Haut-Brion, which was bought by the Dillon family in 1983). For all its earthiness, Haut-Brion has always been more about nuance than power. (The 100-point Parker-rated 1989 being a turbocharged exception.) It is the first growth of poets and lovers, as opposed to, say, CEOs and trophy collectors.

More so than any other first growth, Haut-Brion maintains its unique character from vintage to vintage—look for unheralded vintages like '81, '83, '91, and '94 on wine lists or at auctions. I have yet to be disappointed by a bottle of Haut-Brion. Unlike its northerly peers, it can be delicious in its youth, and yet it improves for decades, becoming—like a person of strong character, like Joan Dillon or Jean Delmas, I suspect—more idiosyncratic with the passing years, more unmistakably itself. More perticular, as Pepys would say.

Before I'd ever tasted Salon, I was entranced by the name, evocative as it is of the intersection of the social life with the life of the mind—of George Sand entertaining Flaubert and Turgenev, or Gertrude Stein hosting Picasso and Hemingway. The literal fact is that Salon is named for its creator, Eugène-Aimé Salon, who established this tiny Champagne domaine in 1921 after making his fortune as a furrier.

Salon might plausibly claim to be the first cult wine of the twentieth century; it was the house Champagne at Maxim's in the 1920s and '30s and has always been made in such small quantities as to make Cristal seem mass-market by comparison. If you've even heard of it, you probably qualify as a wine wonk.

Honestly, until recently I don't think I'd tasted Salon more than three or four times, although I was never less than mesmerized when I did. Certainly, the rarity (and expense) enhances its mystique, but in my experience, the moment you taste it the question of whether any bottle of Champagne could be worth two hundred bucks will probably cease to be an issue. My first glass of Salon (the 1982, in 1996) reminded me in many ways of my first white truffle, and in fact this pairing is one of the great food-and-wine matches. Risotto, white truffle, Salon. Oh. My. God.

Salon's singularity is the result of several factors. It was the world's first Blanc de Blancs Champagne made entirely from Chardonnay grapes from the midslopes of vineyards in Le Mesnil-sur-Oger, the preeminent village for Chardonnay in the region (and also the home of Krug's Clos du Mesnil). Unlike Krug, the other cult Champagne, it never comes near a barrel, old or new. It is made only in the greatest years. (All the luxury cuvées make this claim, even as they declare vintages in less than stellar years, like '92.) It's generally released some ten years after the vintage (the current vintage is 1996) and in the opinion of connoisseurs is at its best some ten to twenty years after that.

"If Dom Pérignon is the Mercedes of Champagne," says Didier Depond, the effervescent director of Salon, "then Salon is the Ferrari or the Maserati." Most of us may never get the chance to drive either one, but Salon is a relatively accessible luxury and one that needn't be framed by pomp and ceremony, a point that Depond probably wanted to emphasize when he invited me to share a couple of bottles with him at J'Go in Paris—a hip, noisy bistro in the Ninth Arrondissement. I was kind of expecting to drink this august nectar at Ducasse or L'Ambroisie, and Depond is a regular at both these places, but he's also a bullfighting aficionado with a pretentiousness deficit. There's something really invigorating about a great luxury Champagne in an informal setting.

The '95 Salon that we started with was something to savor in itself, full-bodied and incredibly silky in texture, with a mousse of tiny bubbles; but given its stiletto acidity it proved to be a pretty amazing accompanist to a succession of tapas.

Even more intriguing was the 1988, the aromas of which reminded me—nutty as it sounds—of walking through the New England woods in October with a fresh loaf of sourdough bread under my arm. It was incredibly lush in the mouth, younger and fresher than you'd expect from the nose. Depond said we'd be drinking it with the toro course, and I thought tuna belly and Champagne were a very sensible combination. The toro turned out to be a flavorful and earthy piece of bull that had recently perished in the ring. It was first served in a carpaccio version, then sliced and char-grilled, both offerings nicely framed by the toasty, earthy '88 Salon. I'm pretty sure I'll never be confronted with this particular pairing again, but I'll certainly never forget it. Perhaps the point I'm making, courtesy of Depond, is that everything tastes good with Salon—or, perhaps, that in this era of high-low aesthetics, of couture denim and Harley-Davidson motorcycles at the Guggenheim, we shouldn't be too reverent or prissy about great Champagne.

For most of us, Salon will always be something of a special-occasion wine rather than a breakfast, lunch, and dinner staple. But connoisseurs on a budget can experience the prêt-à-porter version of Salon via Champagne Delamotte, which was founded in 1760. Most years, the grapes that in a great year become Salon go instead to its sister winery, both of which are now owned by Laurent-Perrier. Delamotte Blanc de Blancs is a very satisfying substitute for Salon, and an excellent expression of Le Mesnil Chardonnay at less than half the price. The nonvintage brut and the rosé are also extremely good. That's my Christmas present to you this year—the insider's tip. If you can find one, by all means treat yourself to a bottle of Salon for Christmas. And be sure to lay in a case of Delamotte for the new year.

BACCHANALIAN DREAMBOOK

The Wine List at La Tour d'Argent

The most exciting wine book I've read in recent years, without question, is the *carte de vin* at La Tour d'Argent, the renowned Paris landmark on the quai de la Tournelle in the Fifth Arrondissement. Founded in 1582, the restaurant is famous for the views of the Seine from the sixth-floor dining room, for its elite clientele, and for its *caneton pressé,* a.k.a. pressed duck, the millionth of which was served last April to great fanfare. I personally consumed duck no. 999,426, and have the commemorative postcard to prove it. The more exciting number, to my mind, is the half million plus bottles that reside in its wine cellar. The five-pound document that catalogs these riches is pure porn to wine geeks.

The keeper of this legacy is David Ridgway, an Englishman with twenty-five years of service at La Tour d'Argent, who puts me in mind of Bob Hoskins playing a French sommelier. It's hard to believe anyone younger than Methuselah could have tasted all the wines on the list, let alone have perfect and detailed recall of each of them, but after quizzing him for a few hours last spring I'm inclined to believe Ridgway has and does. His manner, on first encounter, seemed to combine a bit of British reserve with Gallic institutional pride bordering on hauteur. (No, he will not be shaking your hand and saying, "Hi there, my name's Dave.") After an hour or so, I began to see the passionate fanaticism of a true Bacchanalian initiate.

It was Easter lunch; I had planned to attend Sunday Mass at Notre-Dame but was discouraged by the throngs. Fortunately, my table commanded an excellent view of the cathedral; I was able to hear the bells if not the homily. And the meal, with its accompaniment of wines, was pretty close to a religious experience.

My friend and I were greeted by the late proprietor Claude Terrail, an octogenarian wearing a perfectly draped Huntsman suit and shod in purple velvet slippers with the toes sawed off to reveal his socks—an ensemble that seemed emblematic of his public personality, combining courtly formality with self-deprecating humor. Terrail talks about Clark Gable and Ernest Hemingway as if they had just left the room. The guests that Sunday were mostly Parisian families and American tourists; for us, the big stars were down in the cellar.

With a certain kind of customer—rich American collectors who come specifically to plunder the stores of rare Burgundies from Coche-Dury and Henri Jayer, for instance—one can imagine sommelier Ridgway keeping his own counsel. "Americans can be a little too obsessional," he says. "But when they relax they can be the most knowledgeable." And if you're not knowledgeable—Ridgway shows his softer side. When an American at a nearby table remarks that the wine list is daunting, Ridgway says, "That's why I'm here," in the sommelier equivalent of a soothing bedside manner. "Tell me how much you want to spend" is his straightforward advice for the novice. And if the sight of Ridgway in his tuxedo intimidates you, keep in mind that this is a guy who told me that what he liked best about school was getting drunk at the end of the term.

With the exception of Ports, the cellar at La Tour d'Argent is stocked exclusively with French wines, with a special emphasis on Burgundy, that most ethereal and temperamental of all beverages. The list opens with a hundred-odd pages (they're unnumbered) of *vin de Bourgogne rouge,* including twenty-three vintages of Romanée-Conti stretching back to 1945 and ten vintages of Jayer's Cros Parantoux, including the 1990 for 410 euros. These are some of the reasons Burghounds from around the world jump on planes to Paris for the weekend. Bargain hunters like myself will find a huge selection of modestly priced mature Burgundies, like the '85 Pousse d'Or Clos de La Bousse d'Or Volnay for 105 euros, or the 1990 Ecard Savigny les Beaune aux Serpentières for 94 euros, both of which Ridgway gently steered me toward.

"I get more excited by Burgundy," Ridgway says, relaxing after lunch with a glass of 1947 Armagnac in his tiny windowless office down in the labyrinthian cellars, beneath the quai de la Tournelle. "It's a more living wine." It's also a relative bargain since he buys direct from the domaines—something that's not possible in Bordeaux, with its long-standing negotiant system. Every Monday Ridgway and some of his staff visit a different wine region to taste and hunt for new treasures.

The staggering collection of white Burgundies (Lafon, Coche-Dury, d'Auvenay, Raveneau) provides hundreds of complementary matches to the classic pike quenelles. When I selected the pike for my first course, Ridgway hooked me up with an '83 Drouhin Puligny-Montrachet Caillerets, all honeyed flesh around a core of limestone. The signature pressed duck, an extremely rich, *ancien-cuisine* concoction—the sauce is thickened with the blood of three-week-old ducklings—is probably most easily matched with one of the thousands of Bordeaux or Rhônes on the list, like a '75 Meyney for 136 euros or an '81 Beaucastel for 184. For a special occasion, there's a '47 Pétrus (14,680 euros) or '61 Mouton (8,342 euros). You'll definitely want Ridgway's advice if you're eating the duck and drinking Burgundy. This is even more true of the duck à l'orange, a tricky dish for dry reds, though the version served here is less sweet than many.

La Tour d'Argent's dedication to the wine drinker's pleasure is perhaps best reflected by the number of bottles that are unavailable for immediate drinking; recent, immature vintages are listed without price, alongside the phrase *en vieillissement*. They are maturing. Want to drink a '96 Bordeaux? You'll have to wait. La Tour d'Argent is one of the few restaurants in the world that truly sells no wine before its time. Wish I could think of an American restaurant of which I could say the same.

Part Six

MATCHES MADE IN HEAVEN

What's so exciting about eating a cow? She stands all day chewing, waiting to be led into the slaughterhouse. That's not exciting food. But a wild thing swimming in the water—now that's *passionnant!*

—Gilbert Le Coze

Since Brittany-born siblings Maguy and Gilbert Le Coze brought their fishy act to New York in 1986, no restaurant has done more to elevate and celebrate the role of seafood in this country than Le Bernardin, the four-star midtown temple to Poseidon, which consistently captures the top food rating in Zagat and earned Alain Ducasse's vote as the best fish restaurant in America. Where better to ask the question, What do you drink with fish? And whom better to ask than Michel Couvreux, the diminutive, dynamic sommelier? In a puckish mood, Couvreux likes to flout conventional wisdom and pair chef Eric Ripert's baked red snapper in a spicy-sour Puerto Rican *sancocho* broth with a powerful red such as Jean-Luc Colombo's 1999 Cornas Les Méjeans. But he is the first to admit that white wine is the default setting for seafood—and to argue for the complexity of whites—or, as some of us prefer to call them, golds and silvers.

The iconographers of the vast right-wing conspiracy have demonized white wine as the drink of the effete Martha's Vineyard liberal elite; even self-professed wine enthusiasts like myself often regard white wine as, at best, foreplay, much the way some carnivorous gourmands have regarded fish—as mere prelude to the crimson climax of the menu. Poor misguided bastards. They've probably never eaten at Le Bernardin, never experienced the electric epiphany of Ripert's meaty steamed wild striped bass with a pineapple-lime nage, paired with a racy, stony 1985 Ampeau Meursault Les Perrières. Wimpy? I think not. Just about the only thing more exciting than experiencing this epiphany in the serene dining room of Le Bernardin—a cross between a Zen teahouse in Kyoto and a teak-lined corporate boardroom—is fighting a big striper on a fly rod while standing on the deck of a skiff in eight-foot swells.

The simple fact is that eight out of ten sea creatures prefer white wine to red, in part because the bright acidity of white wine acts like lemon juice in highlighting the flavor, particularly of white-fleshed fish. "Some people say white wine is boring," Couvreux marvels, a look of boyish astonishment on his face. "This is simply not true. The purity, the complexity, the minerality of great white wine ... " He shrugs Gallically, rubbing what is left of his dark hair as if to say, What more can one say?

If Couvreux, who was sommelier at three-star L'Arpège in Paris, were limited to one wine for all fish, it would undoubtedly be white Burgundy. "Puligny-Montrachet, Chassagne-Montrachet, and Mersault," he says, "account for almost half of our sales." For all the Asian spices, and the Spanish influence of Ripert's childhood in Andorra, this is a French restaurant, after all. And the fact is, the complex, neurasthenic Chardonnays of the Côte d'Or, with their subtle fruit, their racy acidity, and their trilling minerality, are about as fish-friendly as any wine in the world. At Le Bernardin, you can get a 2001 Chassagne from Michel Niellon for $125, or a '92 Montrachet from Etienne Sauzet for $1,000 (not bad for one of the greatest makers and one of the greatest vintages of the greatest white vineyard in the world). Couvreux generally reserves the big, buxom New World Chardonnays for lobster: "With its rich texture and its heavy, almost meaty flavor, lobster can stand up to the fruit and the oak of wines like Kistler Les Noisetiers or Peter Michael."

In the eight years that he has been the sommelier at Le Bernardin, Couvreux has developed some rules of thumb that can be applied in the real world, for those of us who, unlike a corporate lawyer of my acquaintance, can't manage to dine daily at Le Bernardin. Most important, what I call the lover/fighter rule: "Sometimes you want the wine to match the food, or the sauce, and sometimes the wine must stand up to the food. Zey must challenge each ozer; zey must fight." For example, in the latter category, Couvreux likes to offset heat with sweetness, as when he pairs Ripert's hamachi tartare with wasabi and a ginger-coriander emulsion with a 2003 Chateau Ste. Michelle Eroica Riesling from Washington State. "With spicy dishes I like Riesling with a little residual sweetness. The sugar balances out and fights the spices."

When fish is served in richer sauces, Couvreux concentrates on matching the flavor and texture of the sauce, as with Ripert's poached halibut with a lobster cardamom emulsion, which he pairs with a rich, floral-scented, almost oily Condrieu La Doriane from Guigal. Condrieu, made from the fragrant, glycerol-rich Viognier grape, is one of his secret weapons. For those who still yearn for red wines, heavier sauces involving red wine and mushrooms provide a bridge. Salmon always takes well to Pinot Noir; with Ripert's morel truffle sauce it can handle even a big earthy Burgundy like the 1999 Leroy Gevrey-Chambertin Le Fonteny.

If you're a red-wine-drinking fish lover, you have a role model in chef Eric Ripert, who trained with Joel Robuchon and Jean-Louis Palladin before joining the late Gilbert Le Coze at Le Bernardin in 1991. Like many of his countrymen, Ripert drinks red Bordeaux with just about everything—much to the exasperation of Couvreux. On the other hand, Ripert did admit to me that a 1972 Domaine de la Romanée-Conti Montrachet he drank recently was the most profound wine he has ever had in his life, so there may be hope for him yet.

WHAT TO DRINK WITH CHOCOLATE

Not far from the spot where Romeo secretly married Juliet, in the Valpolicella hills overlooking Verona, I discovered a more fortunate and successful match. I had just finished lunch with Stefano Cesari, the dapper proprietor of Brigaldara, in the kitchen of his fourteenth-century farmhouse, and I was trying to decide if it would be incredibly uncouth to ask who made the beautiful heather-toned tweed jacket he was wearing, when he put some dark chocolates from Perugia in front of me and opened a bottle of his 1997 Recioto della Valpolicella. One hesitates to describe any marriage as perfect, but I was deeply impressed with the compatibility of his semisweet, raisiny red and the bittersweet chocolates. Cesari later took me up to the loft of the big barn and showed me the hanging trays where Corvina and Rondinella grapes are dried for several months after harvest, which concentrates the grape sugars and ultimately results in an intense, viscous wine that, like Tawny Port, Brachetto, and a few other vinous oddities, enhances the already heady and inevitably romantic experience of eating chocolate.

The Cabernet, Merlot, or Shiraz you drank with your steak may get along well with a simple chocolate dessert, especially if the wine is young and the fruit is really ripe, but real chocoholics should check out the dried-grape wines, many of which are fortified—that is, dosed with brandy, in the manner of Port, a process that stops fermentation and leaves residual sugar. "Fortification seems helpful in terms of matching chocolate," says Robert Bohr, the wine director at Cru, in Greenwich Village, which has one of the best wine lists in the country, if not the world. Bohr likes Tawny Port with many chocolate desserts, finding Vintage Port too fruity. (McInerney does too, and advises that some of the best Tawnies come from Australia's Barossa Valley.) But most of all Bohr likes Madeira.

If you were to order the Hacienda Concepción chocolate parfait at Cru, Bohr would direct you to a vintage Madeira like the 1968 d'Oliveiras Boal. Madeira has become so unfashionable in the past century that many putative wine lovers have never tasted it, but I'm sensing the stirrings of a cult revival spearheaded by supergeeks like Bohr. The sweeter Malmsey style seems to be best suited to chocolate desserts. And by chocolate, I mean, of course, dark chocolate. Milk chocolate should be consumed only by day, if at all, and accompanied by milk.

The cough-syrupy Umbrian *passito* wine is made in the same fashion as Recioto from the mysterious and sappy Sagrantino grape. These powerful, sweet reds seem to have originated as sacramental wines, and they continue to inspire reverence among a small cult of hedonists, myself among them. This practice of drying grapes goes back thousands of years; there are references to drying wine grapes prior to fermentation in Homer and Hesiod. ("When Orion and Sirius come into mid-heaven," Hesiod advises in *Works and Days,* "cut off all the grape clusters and bring them home. Show them to the sun for ten days and ten nights.") I like to imagine that these dried-grape wines resemble those that were drunk at Plato's symposium or Caligula's bashes—although chocolate wouldn't appear in Europe until the sixteenth century, Columbus having stumbled upon a stash of cacao beans on his fourth and last voyage to the New World.

Two of the finest wines for chocolate, Maury and Banyuls, come from remote Roussillon in France's deep southeast. These so-called *vins doux naturels* are made (mostly) from late-picked Grenache grown on steep, terraced, wind-scoured hillsides near the Spanish border. The standard-bearing Banyuls estate is Domaine du Mas Blanc, one of the world's most famous obscure domaines. I first tasted this wine at JoJo, Jean-Georges Vongerichten's pioneering New York bistro, alongside the warm Valrhona chocolate cake, a nearly erotic experience that I try to re-create at least once a year. (And I'm a guy who doesn't usually even bother with dessert.)

Banyuls's neighboring appellation Maury also produces a chocolate-loving *vin doux.* The village cooperative makes the classic example; I recently had, alongside Le Bernardin's warm chocolate tart, a 1929 that was spectacular, with lots of caramel, date, coffee, and vanilla flavors, plus an oxidized Sherry note, which the French and Spanish call *rancio.* The finest estate in Maury is Mas Amiel (which once traded hands in a card game), producers of several cuvées of heady Maury, including one raised in the traditional manner of the region, spending a year outdoors in huge glass demijohns, exposed to the extremes of the Roussillon climate. The demand for these labor-intensive wines, like that for most sweet wines, has been static in the past few decades (Mas Amiel is increasingly focusing on the production of dry table wines), and prices remain modest when compared with Vintage Port or Sauternes.

America's answer to Banyuls and Recioto is late-harvest Zinfandel—a fairly rare, sweet style of Zin that is eminently delicious with chocolate, the darker and more bitter the better. This is a good general rule: chocolate with a high cocoa content and a lower milk and sugar content is the most complex, intense, and wine-friendly. As for the desserts, the more complicated they get, the harder they will be to match. Chocolate already has some five hundred flavor compounds— how many more do you need? A chocolate soufflé is a beautiful thing, but it's hard to improve upon a simple piece of Valrhona, Bernachon, or Scharffen Berger dark chocolate, unless of course you pour a Madeira or a Maury alongside it.

PROVENÇAL PINK

Not the least pleasure of wine is its mnemonic quality—its madeleine-like ability to reawaken previous pleasures, to transport us back in time and place. If I fail, as seems likely, to make it physically to Provence this summer, I will revisit it often in memory—whenever I open a bottle of rosé. Rosé is made in most of the world's wine regions, but in my mind it will always be evocative of southern France, of the fragrant villages between Avignon and Cannes, and of the food of that region.

Several of my most memorable meals have been washed down with rosé, none more satisfying than a lunch at a tiny restaurant near the village of Apt. I'd just spent two days tasting the '98 vintage in Châteauneuf-du-Pape—huge red tannic monsters. My mouth was still puckered with tannin as I set out with a friend that morning from Avignon for a little R & R— honest, wine tasting is *work*—in Peter Mayle country. Someone had recommended a stop at Mas Tourteron, but I don't recall any great expectations when we finally disembarked in the dusty parking lot in the midst of a cherry orchard after innumerable wrong turns. (Forget about your Michelin map in Provence—it doesn't work.) We entered the gate of a walled-in courtyard that dwarfed the farmhouse to which it was attached.

The courtyard was hushed and deserted, a few rough farm tables scattered on the lawn among the trees. Birdcages were mounted on the walls and the trees. The fragrance from scattered flowerbeds was almost narcotic. The pleasant spell was eventually broken with the arrival of Philippe Baique, the deeply tanned, silver-haired husband of chef Elisabeth Bourgeois; he offered us our pick of the tables and returned with the menus and the wine list, which included superstars from such producers as Guigal and Krug. But we were interested in the local talent. We put ourselves in the hands of the proprietor, who brought out a bottle of rosé and advised us to arm ourselves against the sun with one of the many straw hats that were hanging in the trees around us. Hot and thirsty as I was, I found it hard to imagine that anything had ever tasted so good as that rosé. It hardly needed food, given the continuing suspense in the mouth of the sweet fruit dueling with the citrusy acidity. But it played a strong supporting role with my first course—a dish that I hesitate to call tomato soup since it was actually the Platonic essence of tomato, highlighted with basil and other herbs. The wine continued to shine with the salmon with herbs in parchment, and I was loath to give it up even with the arrival of the clafoutis, made from the cherries that had just come into season.

Baique told us that the producer, Domaine de La Citadelle, was just a few miles away in Ménerbes, and he eventually drove us over to the castle that houses the winery to meet the proprietor, the squirish and impeccably tweeded M. Yves Riusset-Rouard, who made his pile, in part, as producer of the salacious *Emmanuelle* movies. In addition to rosé, M. Riusset-

Rouard makes some impressive Cabernet-based reds, but his most distinctive accomplishment may be the creation of the Corkscrew Museum on the premises, which houses the world's largest collection of these vital implements.

A few days later, at a cliffside restaurant overlooking the Mediterranean in Marseille, I discovered the ultimate food match for Provençal rosé: bouillabaisse. Even if, especially if, you're the kind of girl who thinks she's too sophisticated for rosé, you will be converted by this match. Of course, the Marseillaises—included winemaker Jean-Luc Colombo, who was my dinner partner—claim that you can't get true bouil-labaisse outside of the Mediterranean. The good news is that while no wine will ever taste quite as good at home in Des Moines as it will in, say, the lavender-scented hilltop town of Corbierres, in the age of refrigerated shipping containers it should be pretty much the same beverage.

The wine I was swilling with my bouillabaisse, Mas de La Dame, is one of many good Provençal rosés available in the States. It comes from the Les Baux appellation—the hills south of Saint-Rémy. And if the starkly beautiful landscape around the seventeenth-century farmhouse looks familiar, that may be because van Gogh painted it while he was living in Saint-Rémy. The estate employs the consulting services of Colombo, who races between estates up and down the Rhône Valley in his BMW. Like most Provençal rosés, Mas de La Dame is made from a blend of red wine grapes—in this case, Grenache, Cabernet, and Syrah—which are removed from their pigment-bearing skins before fermentation.

The best-known appellation for Provençal rosés is Bandol,

located on the coast between Marseille and Toulon. Domaine Tempier and Château Pradeaux are my perennial favorites. The Côtes de Provence appellation is the home of the famous Domaine Ott, which comes in that funny Greek-urn-shaped bottle and costs almost twice as much as the average Provençal rosé. But at times, with certain foods, it can seem more inspired than a first-growth Bordeaux, as I seem to recall it did over a lunch with English friends at a restaurant called Tetou on the beach at Golfe Juan. We were celebrating my friend's Simon's birthday. We ate fish soup and langoustines and the Domaine Ott kept coming as the waves lapped the sand and bathers wandered past a few feet from our table. I haven't seen Simon for several years, but whenever I open a bottle of Domaine Ott, as I did recently on a cold day in New York, I think about that afternoon on the beach.

ODD COUPLES

What to Drink with Asian Food

The classic European dishes have their classic wine matches: Bordeaux with rack of lamb, Sauternes with terrine of foie gras, Barolo with *brasato*. But most of us, I suspect, eat moo shu pork and chicken tikka masala more often than we eat beef bourguignonne. Asian cuisines were not developed with indigenous wines, so we can't rely on tradition, but that doesn't mean you have to drink beer—or sake—when you go Asian.

To begin with, let me make a blanket generalization and declare that Champagne goes very well with sushi and most other Japanese food. According to Richard Geoffroy, winemaker for Dom Pérignon, it's a marriage based, in part, on the compatibility of the yeast in the Champagne and the yeast in the soy sauce; plus, the wine's high acidity cuts through the saltiness—as with caviar. For similar reasons, Champagne works well with dim sum. It's more difficult to make generalizations about other Chinese cuisines, given the many regional styles, but most of us are familiar with a hybrid of Cantonese and Szechuan cooking.

I recently celebrated my birthday at Canton, my favorite Chinese restaurant, located in New York's Chinatown. One reason I chose the place was that it allows me to bring my own wine. On the other hand, Cantonese food is not exactly a slam dunk when it comes to wine matching. But I had more hits than misses.

One intuition, increasingly confirmed by experience, is that the white wines of Alsace and Germany often make great companions for Chinese and South Asian dishes—Riesling being especially companionable with Cantonese cooking, as the '99 Barmès Buecher Hengst *grand cru* proved in conjunction with the minced squab wrapped in lettuce leaf. The most exciting match of the birthday dinner was a Zind-Humbrecht Pinot Gris with Peking duck. (Several Alsatian winemakers, including Olivier Humbrecht, had tipped me off to this one. The slight smokiness of the Pinot Gris is amplified by the smokiness of the long-cooked duck.) One thing that makes these wines so successful with somewhat sweet, somewhat spicy food is their residual sugar. Anyone who is horrified at the idea of sweetness—who thinks that the words *dry* and *sophisticated* are synonymous—should get over it. Or drink beer. A touch of sugar, which many Alsatian and German wines have, is the perfect counterpoint to spice; these wines are also inevitably high in acidity, which balances out the sweetness of a sauce like hoisin. When going German, choose a *Spätlese,* a late-picked wine with good body and ripeness.

I also had a red wine success, pairing a '96 Martinelli Jackass Hill Vineyard Zinfandel with the Cantonese beef and onions. I have since had almost unerring satisfaction with (red) Zinfandel and Chinese food, especially Ridge's Lytton Springs (a 70 percent Zin blend), which is widely available. I have no idea why Zinfandel works with such a wide variety of feisty Chinese dishes—like sesame chicken and orange-flavored beef—though I suspect it has to do with the natural exuberance and sweetness of the grape and its low tannins. Try it.

I have always loved Viognier, especially from the Condrieu region of France, but I never really knew what to drink it with—it seems too floral and assertive for most white wine dishes—until I took a suggestion from a waiter at Chiam, a Chinese restaurant in midtown Manhattan. The 2000 Copain Viognier from the Russian River region of California seemed to distinguish itself with every dish—shrimp dumplings, spicy prawns, and sesame chicken—and I have since been converted to Chinese with both French and domestic Viogniers. Indian food is, if anything, even trickier than Chinese. Vindaloo, anyone? (Again, there are many cuisines in the subcontinent, but on these shores generalizations can be made.) I have often drunk Gewürztraminer with Indian food—it's almost a cliché at this point that Gewürz, with its wacky rosewater and lychee nut character, goes with hot food like curries. The principle of balancing sweet and hot serves as a guideline—think of the wine as serving the purpose of a sweet chutney. A slightly sweet Gewürz, even a Vendange Tardive, can stand up to a hotter curry.

I was introduced to a more offbeat partner for Indian flavors by Richard Breitkreutz, the former wine director at three-star Tabla, which specializes in the cuisine of chef Floyd Cardoz's native southern Goa. Breitkreutz brought out a '96 Martinez Bujanda Rioja Finca Valpiedra Reserva with the chicken tikka, eliciting a skeptical hoot from me. But the two seemed made for each other, and the Rioja complemented all the other dishes on the table, including a medium-hot curry. I've since discovered that this was no fluke. Breitkreutz thinks it has something to do with the earthiness of the wine.

With its green and red curries and sweet and spicy combinations, Thai food presents similar challenges. Gewürz is a good place to start, particularly with *gai pad bai krapow*—spicy chicken or beef with onions and basil. Viognier also stands up. And Australian Sémillon from the Hunter Valley seems to work especially well in conjunction with lemongrass and ginger. As for reds, I have had good luck pairing young Australian Shirazes with spicy beef salads and several other dishes. The explanation for this match probably has nothing to do with relative geographical proximity.

Perhaps the most interesting thing about matching wine with Asian food is that it's a relatively new area of inquiry. Many discoveries await the wine geek and the novice alike. Dial up your local takeout, open a few modestly priced bottles, and be prepared for some pleasant surprises.

Part Seven

BIN ENDS

BABY JESUS IN VELVET PANTS

Bouchard and Burgundy

> A great bottle of Burgundy is one of the strongest argu-
> ments we have in favor of wine.... The problem for most
> of us, though, is to find that great bottle of Burgundy.
> —Gerald Asher, *Vineyard Tales*

Back in 1985 I found myself staying at the Chateau Marmont
in West Hollywood at the expense of a large movie studio.
While the Chateau's room service menu was minimal enough
foodwise to satisfy the most demanding anorexics and drug
abusers, it listed a couple dozen old vintages of *grand cru* Burgundy from Bouchard Père et Fils. Visiting repeatedly over
the next few years, I helped deplete this cellar and in the
process developed an ugly Burgundy habit, which has per-
sisted to this day.

Burgundy is a wine for chronic romantics—those for whom
hope perenially triumphs over experience. If you are a sensible person with a family, a full-time job, and a sound belief
in cause and effect, you might want to avoid the Côte d'Or.
Once you've experienced the transport of a great bottle of
Burgundy, you may end your days broke, drooling on Burgundy Wine Company catalogs, offering sexual favors to
sommeliers—all in the vain hope of re-creating that rapture.

Having scared the wimps from the room, let me qualify this gloomy scenario by proposing a reliable source for this particular controlled substance.

Founded in 1731, Bouchard owns more prime vineyards in the Côte d'Or than any other firm. And in many ways, its history is emblematic of the region. Bouchard's headquarters was built on the ruins of the fifteenth-century Château de Beaune, which the family purchased after the French Revolution; the ancient cobwebbed cellars contain what is undoubtedly the world's largest library of old Burgundy vintages, extending to the early part of the last century. Long renowned for its magnificent *grand crus,* by the 1970s the firm was, like Burgundy itself, coasting on its reputation.

In the 1960s and '70s many of the region's famous vineyards had been planted with mutant, high-yielding vines and saturated with fertilizers. The feeble wines from these overworked vineyards were routinely turbocharged with sugar and tartaric acid, with little regard to the strict laws limiting these practices. Worst of all, some Burgundian estates and negotiants routinely labeled and sold lesser village wines from the flats as *premier crus* and *grand crus* from the more prestigious hillside vineyards, as well as wines from the Rhône Valley and elsewhere, making a mockery of the entire appellation system. Although these practices were widespread, the authorities decided to make an example of the biggest fish in Beaune. In October 1987 they descended on Bouchard's headquarters, seizing the cellar book, which documented dubious cellar practices. Bouchard ended up paying a $400,000 fine and was subsequently sold to to Joseph Henriot, the suave, impeccably tailored former president of Clicquot Inc., who also runs his family's domaine in Champagne. Since 1995, Henriot has presided over an extensive overhaul of Bouchard, the results of which were first really showcased in the very good '99 vintage.

Bouchard's vineyard holdings have long been concentrated in the Côte de Beaune, the southern half of the Côte d'Or, home of Burgundy's great whites, including 2.2 acres of Le Montrachet. I was a little disappointed when I first laid eyes on this gently sloping (five-degree) hillside vineyard, the holiest of holies for Chardonnay drinkers. I think I expected it to resemble the Matterhorn. But my sense of awe was restored later when I tasted the '99 Bouchard Montrachet in their cellars. Montrachet is never the fattest or fruitiest Chardonnay on the block, but at its best it has a stony purity that resonates and lingers on the palate as a tuning fork does on the eardrum. And it can develop for decades. I recently had a '61 Bouchard Montrachet at the Manhattan restaurant of the same name; it was incredibly fresh and vibrant and, according to the note I made at the time, reminded me somehow of the prose of Hemingway's "Big Two-Hearted River." An authentic, more affordable version of the Montrachet experience— for those of us who balk at spending three hundred dollars and up for a bottle of wine—can be found in Bouchard's Mersaults and Puligny-Montrachets, which come from neighboring vineyards.

For many years Bouchard's signature red wine has been the Beaune Grèves La Vigne de L'Enfant Jésus, a *premier cru* said by the nuns who once owned the vineyard to produce wine as smooth as the baby Jesus in velvet pants—about as weird an analogy as I've encountered even in the overheated field of wine descriptors. As a former student of Raymond Carver's, let me just add: I like it a lot. Among the best values in Burgundy year in and year out is another Bouchard Beaune—the Clos-de-La-Mousse. Henriot extended the firm's portfolio with the purchase of prime vineyards in the more northerly Côtes de Nuits, home of Burgundy's most prestigious reds. The *grand cru* Bonnes-Mares and the Nuits-Saint-Georges Les Cailles are among the standouts of recent vintages.

Bouchard also bottles wines made from purchased grapes, but it is the estate wines, in which the words *Bouchard Père et Fils* appear in script on top above the vintage, that are the most exciting, coming from Bouchard's own vineyards. The winemaking, supervised by the genial Phillipe Prost, is impeccable. (Note that Bouchard Aîné is another firm entirely.) I hesitate to recommend Burgundy to the general public, but if you're willing to risk your peace of mind in pursuit of one of the most exciting sensory experiences available inside the law and outside of bed, you could do worse than to check in with my old Hollywood friends at Bouchard Père et Fils.

My first buzz was strictly kosher, courtesy of a bottle of Manischewitz Concord grape wine, filched from my neighbor Danny Besser's parents in Chappaqua, New York. It struck me as a wonderful beverage at the time. I fell into a pond but otherwise emerged from the experience unscathed—even exhilarated. Since then I've sampled a few more bottles at seders, and it's one of those guilty pleasures, like Big Macs, that shouldn't necessarily arouse our grown-up derision. But as a wine drinker I've moved on, and so has kosher wine.

Wine has played an important role in Jewish ritual and was produced for thousands of years in Palestine until the Muslim conquest of A.D. 636. "Wine was the constant thread through Jewish festivals," according to *The Oxford Companion to Wine,* "since it is sipped as the Sabbath starts (kiddush) and again when it ends (habdalah) with the blessing 'Blessed are You, Lord our God, King of the universe, who creates the fruit of the vine.' "

Of course, other religions used wine in their rituals, so the Jews distinguished theirs by developing the tradition of kosher wine, whereby only observant Orthodox Jews were allowed to be involved in the production and bottling. The hot wrench that got thrown into the winemaking machinery was the insistence of some rabbinical authorities that kosher wine be boiled, so that heathens wouldn't recognize it as wine and use it in their own rituals. This boiled, mevushal wine, which has lost most of its winelike qualities and all the nuances we talk about when we talk about wine, has for centuries succeeded in scaring off serious wine drinkers.

The kosher wines that are of interest to readers of this column, whether Jewish or gentile, are those that, one way or another, circumvent the mevushal process. (Nonmevushal wines meet strict kosher guidelines, I'm told, provided they're not opened or handled by a nonkosher waiter or sommelier.) The best advice I can give you is to look at the label, and if the wine is mevushal, pass it over. Walk on by. Or, better yet, run.

For Passover and other occasions, there are dozens of serious kosher wines to consider, including wines made under Orthodox supervision at estates like Bordeaux's Léoville-Poyferré and those made at kosher properties in Israel and California.

Yarden, in the Golan Heights, Israel's coolest growing region (we will pass over disputes about sovereignty here), is producing uncooked kosher wines to tempt the heathen palate. Golan is an agricultural paradise, a beautiful and haunted landscape. Site preparation for Yarden's El Rom vineyard in the so-called Valley of Tears—the scene of a massive armored battle in the Yom Kippur War—required the removal of the hulks of 250 Syrian tanks.

Since 1992, Yarden wines have been made by California-born Victor Schoenfeld, a cheerful, nebbishy University of

California at Davis graduate who apprenticed at Mondavi and Chateau St. Jean, and whose wife is a major in the Israeli army. Schoenfeld has been fashioning serious ageworthy kosher Cabernet Sauvignons for the past decade (and has recently taken on Sonoma's Zelma Long as a consultant). At a recent vertical tasting at New York's Union Pacific restaurant, the 1985 was still showing well, and several of the later vintages were outstanding. I can't necessarily recommend the Chardonnay, however—tasting the 2000 vintage, I kept checking my tongue for oak splinters. But Yarden makes a very good Blanc de Blancs, a promising Pinot Noir, and an excellent dessert wine—all of them extremely well priced.

Dalton, based in the Galilee region, makes a beautifully balanced Chardonnay, though I find its reds sweet and cloying. A very promising new source of premium kosher wines in Israel is Recanati, in the Hefer Valley. Cofounded by an Israeli of Italian heritage, the winery is named after the owner's ancestral village. At about twenty dollars, Recanati's 2003 reserve Cab is a steal.

Some of Bordeaux's finest wines are available in limited-quantity kosher versions, thanks in part to the influence of the Rothschild family. Probably the best value for the Passover table is the kosher version of Mouton Cadet from the Baron Philippe de Rothschild group; this premium wine is one of the most widely distributed in the world. The 2000 vintage has produced a wine of real distinction and character.

In America, the finest kosher wines of which I'm aware are being produced under the Baron Herzog label. Herzog has adopted a technique of flash-pasteurizing the juice at

165 degrees; this process seems to have very little, if any, deleterious effect on the finished wine and qualifies the wine to bear the mevushal label. The Special Reserve Chardonnay from the Russian River Valley is usually outstanding, and the reds are well made and well priced. Herzog is owned by the Royal Wine Corporation, which also imports a wide range of kosher wines of wildly diverse quality. Some of them will appeal to oenophiles regardless of their heritage; others will undoubtedly please those who look back fondly on the grape syrup of seders past.

BODY AND SOIL

The quaint, red-roofed town of Wettolsheim, in Alsace, rolls up its sidewalks at dark. One wonders what a sleepless inhabitant might think, looking out his window at three a.m., to see a light in the vineyards—his neighbor François Buecher moving between the rows of vines with a spray gun. And what would the neighbors think if they saw him burying a cow horn packed with manure in the vineyard? By now, one imagines, Wettolsheimers must be used to the eccentric habits of Buecher, who practices a radical form of organic viticulture known as *biodynamique*.

Barmès Buecher is one of dozens of domaines in France that are growing grapes in accordance with the principles of Rudolf Steiner, an Austrian philosopher and polymath, and the founder of the anthroposophical movement. Biodynamic agricultural theory views the farm as a self-sustaining entity within the surrounding ecosystem. A vineyard's ecological balance is determined by the vitality of the soil and the diversity of the organisms living in it, and is subject to the influence of the moon and stars. It's easy to make the theory and some of its practices sound ludicrous, which may explain why many practitioners are reluctant to talk about it. But over the past decade, I've noticed that some of the greatest estates in

France have gone biodynamic. In Burgundy, Domaine Leroy, Domaine Leflaive, and Comtes Lafon—names on anyone's top-ten list—are biodynamic. It makes sense that Burgundy is leading the way in this holistic agricultural approach; in the '60s and '70s many of the great vineyards of the region were bombarded with chemicals in a misdirected attempt to increase production. In Alsace, Zind-Humbrecht, Ostertag, Marcel Deiss, Marc Kreydenweiss, and more than a dozen other estates follow the system. In the Loire, devotees include Domaine Huet of Vouvray and Nicolas Joly of Savennières; and in the Rhône, Chapoutier has racked up dozens of 90-point ratings since it went biodynamic.

Long a force in New Zealand and Australia, biodynamic practice is just beginning to exert an influence in California, as many growers seek ways to lessen their dependence on agrochemicals and sustain the fecundity of their soil. While many vineyards follow the Food and Drug Administration guidelines for organic farming, some California wine-growers are turning to the more rigorous ideas of Steiner's. "Organics is about nonuse of chemicals, while biodynamics is about restoring the soil and putting nutrition back in," says Rob Sinskey, of Robert Sinskey Vineyards, who has adopted biodynamic practices at his Napa vineyards. The Sinskey operation, the Benziger Family Winery in Sonoma, and Frey Vineyards in Mendocino are among a handful of California winemaking estates certified by the Demeter Association, the international body in charge of Steiner's legacy.

The basic principles of biodynamics are as commonsensical as some of its practices are arcane. Advocates argue that long-term use of agrochemicals destroys the microbial and insect life of the soil. When I visited Buecher, he showed me the abundance of earthworms and beetles in his own vineyards, then moved to a neighbor's heavily sprayed plot, where we were unable to find a single living thing. It's the life that we can't see—microorganisms—that is the most important living component of the soil. Proponents like Buecher plausibly claim that biodynamic practices result in better wines that transmit the unique characteristics of the soil and site. "Soil microorganisms bond a plant to the soil," explains Mike Benziger, who started to make the switch to biodynamic farming five years ago and was recently certified. "Microorganisms are the chefs that take a combination of organic and mineral elements in your soil and offer them to the plant in a form it can absorb." Fertilizers short-circuit this process—making the vines act like lockjawed diners at a three-star restaurant, attached to IV drips.

In place of chemicals, biodynamics relies heavily on composting and holistic teas made from nettles and horsetail. Advocates say that building soil and vine health can eliminate the need for insecticides. "We had a Chardonnay vineyard that was problematic," says Rob Sinskey. "We had phylloxera, and we wanted to know why it was spreading so fast. We observed that the soil was dead; there were no earthworms. We started reading up on Steiner, going to Europe." Following biodynamic viticulture slowed the spread of phylloxera, according to Sinskey, and vastly improved grape quality, to the point where the troubled vines now produce his best Chardonnay.

Vine-munching insects are trapped on sticky paper and cremated, their ashes mixed in a solution that is sprayed in a vineyard to repel their fellows. Another preparation sometimes used, horn silica, a.k.a. quartz, is sprayed on vines between three a.m. and eight a.m. at the equinox. Steiner's emphasis on lunar and cosmic rhythms can sound flaky to nonbelievers, but Benziger makes an intuitive case: "The moon moves the oceans, and plants are ninety-eight percent water." Sinskey says that "Steiner refers to the silica spraying as focusing life forces. I see it as refracting light. I don't know how it works. Using silica spray, we've seen sugars leap within twenty-four hours."

Perhaps the most arcane practice of biodynamic viticulture involves the aforementioned burying of manure in cow horns—which Steiner believed are infused with the life force—during the fall equinox. They are dug up in the spring and mixed into a homeopathic spray. Personally, I'd rather drink a wine nurtured with cow horn and nettles than one raised on phosphates and insecticides. The theory, if correct, suggests that biodynamic wines should taste better, and more site specific, in the long run, in addition to being safer, a conclusion that seems to be borne out by the recent wines of growers like Leroy, Leflaive, Zind-Humbrecht, and Chapoutier. But not all biodynamic wines are excellent: Nicolas Joly, of Coulée de Serrant, seems indifferent to the winemaking, as opposed to the winegrowing, process; his recent wines have often been oxidized and downright weird.

Master of Wine Jancis Robinsion, who recently compared the biodynamic and conventional cuvées of Leflaive's wines, says, "I do think that successful biodynamically grown wines do taste different—wilder, more intense, and dangerous—hunting dogs rather than lapdogs, if you like."

"I'm doing it because I think it produces great wines," says Benziger, whose Sonoma Mountain estate wines are well worth seeking out. "I don't want people to buy it because it's biodynamic. I'm also hoping this property will be taken over by my kids, and I want to be able to hand them over a piece of property that's increasing in health, not dying."

Not too long ago, in a faraway place now best known as
Middle Earth, a wine was born. New Zealand Sauvignon
Blanc appeared suddenly, as if it had sprung fully formed
from Zeus's head, and in the past decade it has taken its place
alongside Barossa Shiraz and Napa Cabernet as a kind of
instant classic. It was as though the Kiwis figured out how to
bottle Kiri Te Kanawa's voice. From this distance it appears
that those few of her compatriots who weren't employed as
extras on *Lord of the Rings* were busy planting vines. That was
Act One. Act Two is still getting under way.

For those of you who missed Act One, here is a précis: in
1985 David Hohnen, owner of Cape Mentelle Vineyards in
the Margaret River region of Western Australia, flew to New
Zealand, convinced that the cool climate of the South Island
could produce great Sauvignon Blanc. In fact, Montana, a big
company based on the North Island, had already ventured
south to plant Sauvignon in Marlborough in '76, and its
early bottlings were promising. Hohnen met winemaker Kevin
Judd, hired him on the spot, and bought land in the Marlborough district, on the northeast corner of the island. Within a
year the first vintage of Cloudy Bay Sauvignon Blanc, made
from locally purchased grapes, was creating a buzz and winning prizes in Australia and the United Kingdom.

Within a decade Cloudy Bay had spawned numerous imitators and had helped create a new style of wine. For some reason, Sauvignon Blanc grown in cool, sunny Marlborough tastes like nothing else—certainly not like the lean, stony, lemony Sauvignons from Sancerre and Pouilly-Fumé. These Marlborough Sauvignons are fruit cocktails suggestive of lime, mango, grapefruit, and, especially, for those who have encountered them, gooseberries. Nearly everything on Carmen Miranda's hat—along with a few renegade vegetables, like asparagus and bell pepper. What holds it all together is a wire-mesh foundation of acidity that comes from the long, cool growing season in this marginal climate.

At this point, Marlborough Sauvignon Blanc is a category unto itself, so successful that it is inspiring emulation in South Africa and South America. It's hard to go wrong buying a bottle, most of which fall in the ten- to twenty-dollar range. Brancott, Seresin, Villa Maria, and Thornbury are some of the more reliable producers. Chardonnay also does well in Marlborough, producing lean, racy versions. The most exotic Chardonnay seems to come from the warmer North Island, around Auckland. The Chards from Kumeu River Wines, founded in 1944, have developed a cult following in Great Britain and Australia over the years and are well worth seeking out, as are the big Chardonnays of nearby Matua.

Pinot Noir is supposed to be the great red hope of this cool country. For years we've been hearing the buzz about the imminence of great Pinot, particularly from the Martinborough region. More recently, Central Otago has emerged as the great new *terroir* for Pinot. I have tasted some good ones from both regions—Martinborough Vineyard and Felton Road are worth seeking out—but for now the vines are young and Pinot Noir is, let's face it, a bitch.

One of the more promising developments in Act Two is taking shape in Hawke's Bay, under the auspices of a new winery called Craggy Range, founded in 1999, which is producing single-vineyard bottlings of Sauvignon Blanc as well as red grape varietals—a new approach in New Zealand. American-born, Australian-based mogul Terry Peabody traveled the globe for seven years looking for the perfect spot to convert a fortune based on waste management into a world-class wine estate. Peabody settled on Hawke's Bay, where vines have been grown since the nineteenth century, and hooked up with New Zealand viticulturalist Steve Smith, a cheerful polar bear of a man who, for all his antipodean mateyness, is a Master of Wine and a rabid Francophile.

The first act of the New Zealand wine story relied heavily on technology, but Smith is a *terroir* freak, obsessed with expressing the individual characters of specific vineyard sites. Craggy Range's first offering was a single-vineyard Sauvignon that was more polished and subtle than the typical Marlborough SB, if still recognizably New Zealand. This past year the winery released a stunning Puligny-like single-vineyard Chardonnay called Les Beaux Cailloux.

Hawke's Bay's Bordeaux-like maritime climate had inspired earlier growers to plant Cabernet and Merlot. A warm and rocky district called the Gimblett Gravels winegrowing district is beginning to look ideal for Bordeaux grapes; a '98 Merlot from the area, from C. J. Pask, won the gold medal in the Bordeaux red class at the 2000 International Wine Challenge.

Craggy Range is about to release several small-production reds from this area, including a rich, silky Cabernet Franc–Merlot blend called Sophia and a blockbuster Syrah. If these wines are any indication, some of the protagonists of New Zealand's second act will be red.

Talking to some New Zealand winemakers one picks up a certain impatience, even embarrassment, about the spectacular success of Sauvignon Blanc. For some reason I'm reminded of John Grisham's recent attempt to go upmarket with his "literary" novel, *A Painted House*, and of Paul McCartney's symphony. I only hope that Kiwi winemakers, as they explore and develop new styles and new grapes, keep playing to their strengths, and our thirst. The late Auberon Waugh, who was pretty stingy with his compliments, once said, "It's very difficult to be best in the world at anything, but New Zealand has achieved that distinction with Sauvignon Blanc."

Part Eight

BUBBLES AND SPIRITS

NUMBER TWO AND BITCHING LOUDER

Armagnac

I'm not a big drinker of spirits these days. Wine provides more nuance and interest at the expense of fewer brain cells. But I happened to acquire an interest in Armagnac during trips to Bordeaux, where it's often served after dinner at the great châteaux, and at the renowned bistro La Tupina, where wine merchants and châteaux owners savor old Armagnac vintages after washing down a roast chicken with a bottle of Pauillac. Over time I came to appreciate the complexity and variety of France's No. 2 brandy, as well as the sense of completion and contemplation inspired by an after-dinner snifter. "At its best," claims British spirits expert Nicholas Faith, "Armagnac offers the drinker a depth, a natural sweetness, and a fullness unmatched by even the finest cognac."

Everyone in the heavily forested Gascony region, a hundred miles south of Bordeaux, will tell you that Armagnac is France's oldest spirit, first distilled as early as 1411. Cognac got off to a much later start, but that town's position on the Charente River allowed for easy transport and eventual international renown. The brandy of Armagnac remained something of a local cult, and it was often credited for the great longevity of the inhabitants. While Cognac production is concentrated in a handful of wealthy firms, Armagnac is still largely an artisanal product crafted by feisty individuals like Martine Lafitte of Domaine Boingnères.

With her jet-black helmet of hair, her big Valentino tortoiseshell glasses, and her tiger-striped sweater and tight white pants, Lafitte might be the proprietress of a beauty salon or travel agency. Here in the homeland of d'Artagnan and foie gras, I was expecting someone a little more . . . rustic. One is tempted to say that she is not the typical Armagnac producer, except that the more people you talk to here, the more you realize that this is a region of Gallic individualists who passionately disagree about how to make *le vrai Armagnac*. In this regard, the region is more like Burgundy than Bordeaux—a place of small plots and contentious peasants going their own way, squabbling among themselves about *le vrai Armagnac* even as they insult the intregrity of that other French brandy that fills duty-free shops around the globe.

The Boingnères estate, in the Bas-Armagnac region, which has been in Lafitte's family since 1807, comprises about fifty acres—not much when you consider that her Armagnac is in demand from Tokyo to New York. Half of that acreage is planted with the Folle Blanche grape, which is Lafitte's particular passion. Folle Blanche is more difficult to raise than Ugni Blanc and Colombard, two more common grape varieties, and hence is on the decline, but to her mind it produces the richest and most aromatic Armagnac. Lafitte's father was one of the great champions of Folle Blanche, but many of his neighbors disagreed with his strident advocacy of it as the true grape of Armagnac, preferring the more forgiving varieties. One day he arrived at his *chai* to find a cross of flowers from the cemetery in front of the cellar door. "It's a tough region," Martine Lafitte says proudly, getting a last drag on her Craven A before she takes me in to the cellar. "We fight for our beliefs."

Lafitte shows me the old-style alembic—twin copper towers wherein the wine is heated and evaporated in the winter, following the harvest. She distills to about 49 percent alcohol, producing a more flavorful spirit than the 70 percent typical in Cognac. The spirit gains additional flavor and mellowness in the oak casks, where it may develop for decades. Unlike some makers, Lafitte doesn't water it down to 40 percent when it's bottled.

Regulations for the region allow Armagnac to be sold in as little as two years, but these young brandies are to be avoided at all costs. Five-year-old Armagnac can be labeled VO, VSOP, or *réserve*. But the best Armagnacs are the older vintages, which are seldom bottled before ten years of age. Laubade, one of the larger domaines in Armagnac, has thousands of barrels of old Armagnacs mellowing (and evaporating) in a series of cellars on the slope below its tiled 1850 manor house. At Laubade they believe the wood is just as important as the grape, and they get much of their oak from a nearby forest and then stack it and dry it for several years before cooperage. Laubade's Armagnacs are produced largely from the Baco grape, which many believe has greater aging potential than Folle Blanche. (Even Mme. Lafitte grants Baco the virtue of longevity.) In their first twenty years of life, these don't show the complexity of Folle Blanche–based Armagnacs, but they really start to sing when they hit the age of majority.

Tasting through vintages back to 1934, I was impressed

by the increasing complexity and depth of the older spirits, although, as with fine wines, some vintages are notably superior to others—the 1947, in this case, being my hands-down favorite.

The practice of vintage dating, which is not followed in Cognac, has made Armagnac increasingly popular, especially on our own vintage-conscious shores. Laubade is one of the few makers that have sufficient stocks of old vintages to make them widely available in the United States, but there are many small makers who are worth seeking out. Most of the best are concentrated in the westernmost Bas-Armagnac region and include some of my favorites: Château de Briat, Laberdolive, Château de Lacquy, and Château du Tariquet. Part of what makes Armagnac so engaging is that there are dozens of makers producing rich and complex brandies that turn up in our restaurants and liquor stores, and any number of these spirits will provide a memorable and contemplative coda to a meal.

WHITE ON WHITE

Blanc de Blancs Champagne

The unspoiled little town of Le Mesnil-sur-Oger sits almost smugly in the center of the rolling hills of Champagne's Côte des Blancs. BMWs and Mercedeses race through the narrow streets, driven by some of the world's most prosperous small farmers. These happy Frenchmen grow Chardonnay grapes in *grand cru*–designated plots on the chalky hillside, their fruit destined for some of the world's greatest Champagnes. Hidden in the center of town, behind eighteenth-century houses, is the fossil-strewn Clos du Mesnil vineyard, probably the most hallowed piece of ground in Champagne, owned by the house of Krug.

Blanc de Blancs, literally "white of whites," is made from Chardonnay grapes. Don't groan. "A lot of my customers say, 'But I hate Chardonnay,'" says Charles Stanfield, the tattooed, Sub-Zero-sized chief of sparkling wines at Sam's Wines in Chicago. "I tell 'em, 'Hey, get over it, there's Chardonnay and there's Chardonnay. Blanc de Blancs is the Chablis of Champagne—very crisp, very dry.'" Stanfield's customers never disagree with him, at least not to his face. And neither should you. For one thing, he's a Chevalier de l'Ordre des Côteaux de Champagne. He's also the Mr. T of wine retailing. He loves Blanc de Blancs. So should you.

The typical Champagne is made from a blend of Pinot Noir, Pinot Meunier, and Chardonnay. Not a bad recipe. But if you ever taste a mature Clos du Mesnil or a Taittinger Comtes de Champagne, you will realize that there is something magical about the Chardonnay grapes of this northerly region. Many hard-core Champagne drinkers believe that 100 percent Chardonnay Champagne can achieve greater vinous intensity and longevity than Pinot-heavy blends. Sipping a 1982 Salon or a 1988 Dom Ruinart Blanc de Blancs could forever destroy your preconceptions about white wine being light in body or delicate in flavor. Imagine hearing Beethoven's Ninth blasted through a stack of Marshall amps. These are wines; they are meant to be aged, and to be sipped with food. Big food. That said, there are lighter, leaner styles of Blanc de Blancs that make the ideal aperitif—for instance, the Blanc de Blancs of Michel Turgy, a small grower in Mesnil, which truly remind me of Chablis, with its chalky minerality. (The Côte des Blancs' Kimmeridgian chalk is part of the same geological formation that surfaces in Chablis.)

While most of us look to the big, famous Champagne houses for our bubbly, an increasing number of smaller makers have begun to appear in recent years, and American importers have begun to seek them out. Many of the best Blanc de Blancs come from small proprietors like Larmandier-Bernier, Jacques Selosse, A. R. Lenoble, De Sousa & Fils, J. Lassalle, and P. Lancelot-Royer. Most of these wines are made in small quantities, from villages like Avize and Cramant, which are rated *grand cru,* the highest designation in Champagne's grading system. (If you see that term on the label, it tells you the wine is 100 percent *grand cru*.) While the styles vary, the quality is impeccable, and even wine snobs can appreciate the reverse snobbery of a relatively unknown label. I suspect that boutique Champagnes like these are the wave of the future in Champagne—the bubbly equivalent of cult Cabs.

Midsized producers like Delamotte, Deutz, and Jacquesson also make very good Blanc de Blancs. Delamotte gets first refusal on the grapes rejected by Salon—makers of perhaps the most exotic Champagne in the world. It is produced only in exceptional years from severely pruned, grandfatherly old vines on the midslope of *grand cru* vineyards in Mesnil. (I can't confirm if the grapes are harvested one at a time by blond virgins dressed in gossamer, but I wouldn't be at all surprised.) In the '20s, Salon achieved renown as the house wine at Maxim's, and has since become a password among true Champagne freaks.

One hundred percent sparkling Chardonnay is made elsewhere, including California. Schramsberg's Blanc de Blancs has always been the most interesting and Champagne-like example to me. Mumm's Cuvée Napa makes a pleasant, affordable Blanc de Blancs, but most American versions are too fruity for my palate. Francis Ford Coppola has just put out a Hawaiian Punch of a Blanc de Blancs, named after his daughter Sofia—a nice little quaff for a summer picnic, but a long way from Mesnil.

Like regular bubbly, Blanc de Blancs comes in both vintage bottlings and blends of different years. The vintage to buy, if you choose to spend the money, is '96. The '98 and '99 aren't quite as rich and powerful. The *tête de cuvée* superluxury wines are released much later—the current Clos de Mesnil as of spring '06 is the mind-blowing '95. Salon's latest release seems to be the exquisitely complicated '96. And I have seen both the '88 and '90 Ruinart in stores recently—relative bargains at anything near one hundred dollars. But there are also many excellent nonvintage Blanc de Blancs, starting at around thirty dollars.

So have a blanc Christmas. And a blanc New Year.

MONK BUSINESS

The Secrets of Chartreuse

The history of wine and spirits in Europe is inextricably, some would say excessively, bound up with that of the monastic orders of the Catholic Church; by the end of the Middle Ages, asceticism had become nearly synonymous with dipsomania in the popular imagination. The Cistercian, the Benedictine, and the Carthusian orders all contributed to the preservation and development of viticulture, winemaking, and distillation. Among the most glorious examples of the symbiosis of spirits and the spiritual life is the mysterious elixir created by the Order of Chartreuse, the Carthusians, one of the oldest religious orders in Christianity.

The order was founded in 1084 by the scholarly ascetic Bruno in the shadow of the Chartreuse Mountains near Grenoble. In 1605, the monks at a Carthusian monastery in Vauvert received the gift of a manuscript titled "An Elixir of Long Life" from the marshal of artillery for King Henry IV. Already ancient when it came into the possession of the monks, this manuscript has a history as eventful as that of the Ark of the Covenant as narrated by George Lucas. The formula contained therein was so complex that it was more than a hundred years before the apothecary at the order's headquarters in Chartreuse finally unraveled its mysteries.

The first batch of the medicinal beverage that came to bear the name Chartreuse was created in 1737, and rapidly gained popularity in the region.

In the wake of the French Revolution, members of religious orders were forced into exile. The Carthusians fled in 1793, after making a copy of the manuscript and entrusting that copy to one monk, who was allowed to remain in the monastery, and the original to a second monk, who was eventually arrested by the authorities and sent to prison in Bordeaux. Miraculously, he was not searched and managed to pass the manuscript along to a supporter, who smuggled it back to Chartreuse to a third monk, who was hiding near the monastery. Convinced that the order was finished, this monk sold the manuscript to a pharmacist in Grenoble, who was unable to understand the complex recipe. When Napoleon issued an order that all medical formulas be sent to the minister of the interior, the pharmacist obliged. The recipe was promptly rejected and sent back to him. When he died, his heirs donated the manuscript to the monks, who had returned to the monastery in 1816.

The Chartreuse monks might have hoped that history had finally passed them by, until, in 1903, the French government nationalized the distillery, once again expelling the monks, who repaired to Spain with their precious manuscript. They built a new distillery in Tarragona, and another in Marseille, both of which continued to produce the genuine Chartreuse. The government, meanwhile, sold the Chartreuse trademark to a group of distillers, who marketed a beverage that bore no relation to the original, and who went bankrupt in 1929.

Shares of the now worthless stock were bought up by friends of the order and presented to the monks, who thereby regained possession of the Chartreuse trademark. No sooner had they returned to their monastery, however, than an avalanche roared down the mountainside and destroyed the distillery. A new distillery was built in nearby Voiron, although the selection and blending of the herbs and botanicals is still performed at the monastery by three monks entrusted with the secret recipe.

Chartreuse has inspired a cult of secular devotees over the centuries. Its mystique was probably sealed early in the past century with the endorsement of the ultimate host, Jay Gatsby, who, according to his biographer, Nick Carraway, served the drink at his glittering parties on Long Island. I find it stimulating to contemplate this history while passing a glass of Chartreuse under my nose; the survival of the recipe, with its obscure origins, seems nothing short of miraculous. Equally stimulating are the aromas from the glass, which provide endless opportunities for speculation—one of the reasons that Chartreuse is of interest to wine geeks like myself. The most prominent feature is the anise/fennel/licorice note. Dozens of other nuances tease you as they evanesce on the alcoholic vapors. More than 130 varieties of roots and leaves are allegedly involved in Chartreuse's production (including, according to rumor, wormwood, the active ingredient in absinthe).

My friend Jim Signorelli, a Chartreuse aficionado and movie director, suggests that it's enough just to smell the stuff. Hunter S. Thompson, another Chartreuse devotee, presumably swallowed. Alice Waters, also a fan, can probably parse out more of the herbal aromatics than most of us. Three kinds of Chartreuse are currently produced. Green Chartreuse, the standard, was first adapted from the original recipe in 1764 and weighs in at 55 percent alcohol, slightly mellower than the original elixir of life, which was 71 percent. Milder still is yellow Chartreuse, at 40 percent, first distilled in 1838. A small portion of production is selected for extra aging in wood and is sold in reproductions of the nineteenth-century bottles as VEP *(Vieillissement Exceptionnellement Prolongé)* Chartreuse. Chartreuse benefits from aging. It is possible, especially in France, to find dated bottlings from the distillery in Tarragona, which finally closed in 1989.

Aficionados ascribe various curative properties to the liqueur, which was originally conceived as a life-prolonging medicine. A French winemaker of my acquaintance insists that a blend of one part green and one part yellow Chartreuse is the ultimate hangover remedy, though I haven't yet summoned the courage to test this theory.

TINY BUBBLES

Artisanal Champagnes

If you come to my apartment during holiday season, chances are excellent that you will be served a glass of Egly-Ouriet, Larmandier-Bernier, Jacques Selosse, or some other small-grower Champagne. It's true that my 2005 balance sheet was anything but Cristal-worthy, but, more to the point, these and other small grower-producers are the most exciting trend going in Champagne. If you're lucky enough to score a table at Thomas Keller's Per Se in New York, you'll discover that they're pouring small-grower Champagnes such as Pierre Gimonnet by the glass.

Here at the dawn of the twenty-first century, it is a principle universally acknowledged among grape nuts that great wine is produced in the vineyard—the product of ripe grapes, low yields, and meticulous viticulture that lets the true personality of the vineyard shine through. Except, of course, in Champagne, where farmers who are paid by the ton grow as much as their poor vines will bear, pick the fruit before it's ripe, and sell these wan grapes to vast industrial concerns that mix them all together. The Champenois sometimes cite their unique *terroir* as the reason they make the world's greatest sparkling wine, and yet in practice they usually ignore the nuances of the concept.

After spending a day visiting the headquarters of the Grandes Marques Champagne houses in Épernay, it's refreshing to knock on the door of Francis Egly's little half-timbered house in the village of Ambonnay, where you literally trip over baby toys in the foyer. Egly's mother offers cookies while his wife shouts for Francis out the back door. Egly finally turns up, apologizing for the dirt on his hands—he has been in the vineyards.

I had sought out Egly after an epiphany a few months earlier when the then sommelier at Daniel, Jean Luc Le Dû, handed me a glass of Champagne. "Whoa!" I said. "This is wine!" By which I meant it would be good even without bubbles. And what impressed me when I was tasting with Egly in his spanking-clean new *chai* was that, unlike many young Champagnes in their prebubbly stage, his tasted like good wine. Like most great artisanal growers elsewhere in the world—though like very few growers in Champagne—Egly regularly cuts off up to half the fruit from his vines in midsummer to promote the ripening of the rest.

"When I first started importing these small growers, the people I sold small-domaine Burgundies to had no interest in Champagne," says David Hinkle of North Berkeley Imports. "If we were going to interest these people, it had to be wine first and Champagne second." Terry Theise, the self-proclaimed Riesling wacko, who added small-grower Champagnes to his portfolio in 1997, puts it this way: "Champagne, like any other wine, is fascinating to the extent that it's distinctive." Sounds obvious to me. But the larger Champagne houses would argue that blending the wines of many different villages will create a sum that is greater than its parts.

Champagne is a world unto itself, but some of the best producers are those, like Burgundy-obsessed Egly, who look to other regions for inspiration. Pierre Larmandier, of Larmandier-Bernier, worked in Alsace and Burgundy, where he was surprised to learn that small growers were, if anything, more highly regarded than the large negotiants. With minimal intervention in the cellar, Larmandier-Bernier (not to be confused with Guy Larmandier, another excellent domaine) makes subtle, complex, Chardonnay-based Champagnes, including an all-Chardonnay Blanc de Blancs.

If artisanal Champagne is a movement, Anselme Selosse, also known as "the madman of Avize," might be regarded as its leader—the Angelo Gaja of Champagne. Selosse farms biodynamically, keeps his yields low, and makes his wine with the goal of expressing the character of his vineyard. Avize is located in the Côte des Blancs, where Chardonnay predominates; like Ambonnay, which is Pinot Noir territory, Avize is one of seventeen villages rated *grand cru*.

Jancis Robinson informs me that in this one area at least, we are well ahead of the British: "Americans are lucky to have importers who have scoured the countryside of Champagne in search of these small growers." At present there are more than 130 small-grower Champagnes imported here. In addition to the aforementioned, my short list includes L. Aubry, Gaston Chiquet, René Geoffrey, Pierre Gimonnet, J. Lassalle, Pierre Moncuit, Alain Robert, Michel Turgy, and Vilmart & Cie.

These small producers represent less than 2 percent of the domestic market. But they are being noticed. Moët recently launched three single-vineyard Champagnes.

Smaller isn't always better. I usually have a bottle of Veuve

Clicquot or Perrier-Jouët in my refrigerator, and I happen to be very fond of Krug Grande Cuvée, Bollinger Grande Année, Dom Pérignon, Taittinger Comtes de Champagne, and several other Grandes Marques Champagnes. But this year I'm making more room in my cellar for handcrafted, artisanal Champagnes.

THE WILD GREEN FAIRY

Absinthe

It certainly *feels* illegal—what with all the paraphernalia, the special glasses and spoons, the hookahlike silver-and-crystal fountain at the center of the table, and the ritual aspects of preparation. I'm getting that anticipatory tingle I used to get when drugs were being readied for consumption. We are sitting in a courtyard in the French Quarter of New Orleans. Our connection is Ted Breaux, a compact, muscular New Orleans native with fashionably spiked hair. Breaux is slowly drizzling water from the fountain into a silver funnel balanced on a crystal glass; the emerald liquid in the glass gradually turns milky with the infusion. We are preparing to drink absinthe.

Breaux was cruising the French Quarter one afternoon a decade ago when he spotted some absinthe glasses and spoons in the window of Lucullus, an antique shop dedicated to the culinary arts. "I found it fascinating that there was a special type of glassware and paraphernalia," says Breaux. "It was evidence that the drink existed." An environmental scientist whose family arrived in New Orleans in 1724, Breaux had been curious about the outlawed liqueur since college, when a fellow chemistry major had mentioned it. "I looked it up in the Merck Index. It says that the ingestion of absinthe can cause hallucinations, convulsions, and death. I wondered, What did people get out of it?" That very week he happened to notice Barnaby Conrad's *Absinthe* in a book catalog. He ordered the book, corresponded with the author, and sought out other researchers. An obsession was being born.

Breaux would hardly be the first to become obsessed by the so-called Green Fairy. Some of the greatest artists of the nineteenth and early twentieth centuries came under its spell; writers like Baudelaire, Verlaine, Rimbaud, and Oscar Wilde—a roll call of the premodern decadents—not only drank it but wrote about *le Fée Verte*. Painters like Manet, van Gogh, Gauguin, and Toulouse-Lautrec were devotees of the cult. Absinthe was to Symbolism and Postimpressionism what heroin was to Seattle grunge. Absinthe cultists ascribed mystical, meditative, and even halluncinatory powers to their beverage of choice; opponents saw it as an insidious poison. Both sides agreed that it was something more than just another alcoholic beverage. In 1905, when a Swiss farmer killed his wife and children, allegedly under the influence of absinthe, the calls for prohibiton swelled. Within a decade it was banned throughout Europe and the United States.

Outlaw status has only enhanced the mystique of absinthe over the years. Ted Breaux, for one, was haunted by the myth. After discovering a recipe in an old French book on the subject, he decided to make a batch. "I made it and tried it and I was underwhelmed," he says, sitting in the courtyard behind Lucullus. "It just didn't taste like something that could be that popular. But then a friend of mine popped up with a bottle of vintage Edouard Pernod absinthe." It was as if an amateur

paleontologist had suddenly gotten his hands on a live tricera-
tops. "Finally, I could taste it." At almost the same time, he
came across a second bottle, through his friends at Lucullus.
After he tasted this one too, he says, "I could definitely see
why it was so popular. But the vintage samples were so different from what I made that I got discouraged." Not for long,
however; he had the old samples analyzed in a French lab and
started experimenting again. In the meantime, new European
Union regulations eventually superseded the old national
laws banning absinthe. Through a friend, Breaux got into
contact with a Frenchman who'd bought an old distillery in
the Loire with original absinthe stills, from which he now produces some three thousand bottles a year.

Absinthe is made by distilling herbs in spirits and then distilling the infused spirits again. The color of a properly made
absinthe comes from chlorophyll. Breaux's is far more complex and refined than the other two alleged absinthes I've
tried—a little bitter, with a strong anise flavor in the middle
and a touch of fennel and a bit of mint toward the end. "Some
of the herbs are excitatory and some are sedative," Breaux
says. "You combine the two and it's kind of like a mild herbal
speedball."

This pretty well describes the sensation I am experiencing after a couple of glasses of Breaux's absinthe, which starts
out at 140 proof, before being diluted with water. I feel completely alert and slightly buzzed at the same time, floating
a little above the company even as I am thoroughly present
and engaged. My scalp and fingertips are tingling, whether
because of the slight November chill or the liqueur, I can't be

certain. I notice for the first time the blond flecks in Breaux's hair, which look like tiny flames. I feel that something wonderful is surely about to happen. If anything, this state I'm in reminds me of sitting back after doing a couple of lines and a shot of tequila. But it's somehow different. Breaux is talking about thujone, the chemical compound found in the absinthe plant that is suspected of being the active and potentially dangerous compound in the drink . . . about how cheap imitation absinthe was responsible for ruining the reputation of the real thing . . . about how his house was destroyed in the flooding after Katrina.

Sometime later we float over to the Old Absinthe House, the famous if somewhat shabby bar on Bourbon Street, which specialized in absinthe cocktails before Prohibition. Still later we will drive through the desolate streets of flood-ravaged neighborhoods outside the Quarter. But before that, for a perfect hour or so, I am under the spell of the Green Fairy, listening with keen attention to Breaux and listening to myself talking with unusual precision and grace, or at least so it seemed to me then.

EPILOGUE

WHAT I DRANK ON MY
FORTY-EIGHTH BIRTHDAY

My friend Jancis Robinson, who has celebrated several birthdays with me, asked me to send a report on my forty-eighth, along with wine notes, to be posted on her Web site.

Dear Jancis:

Here's what I drank for my birthday last week. Of course I went through eighteen different plans, several of which involved my cooking. However, when the guest list reached nine I decided to leave the cooking to the pros. I didn't, however, want to leave the wine to the pros—i.e., I didn't want to pay a 200 or 300 percent markup on wines that probably wouldn't be mature anyway—which is the position we find ourselves in when we dine fashionably in New York. So I picked Canton, one of the few places here that I knew wouldn't mind my lugging in a case of wine, plus Riedel glasses. (Actually, I had thirteen bottles, this being my birth date and lucky number.) The cuisine was a challenge—Cantonese. Not your average oenophile's first choice. But I like a challenge.

I started us off with a magnum of 1990 Dom Pérignon, a great vintage for them that has been drinking nicely since its release. Even in this big vintage it's got a feminine delicacy, especially when you compare it to something like Bollinger. Unfortunately, I compared it to 1990 Veuve Clicquot rosé, which seemed a little clumsy following the DP but which came into its own with the Cantonese lobster—very yeasty, which is a good thing with soy sauce, though one bottle was slightly corked. In retrospect, a Chard-based bubbly would have been better. Next we had the '99 Zind-Humbrecht Clos Hauserer Riesling, a beauty: appley, very fat for a Riesling, with a long, sweet finish—definite residual sugar. Near-perfect match for the squab wrapped in lettuce leaf—this dish having a fair amount of sugar itself.

I wanted to go red eventually, and the only thing I could think of for this cuisine was Zinfandel—specifically, monster old-vine Zin in the new superextracted style. Martinelli Jackass Hill to be exact—to my mind the best Zin in America. The '96 was at its peak—the blackberry fruit all still there, tannins melted away. The '99 by contrast, was a hot, brutal monster on its own, but better with the Peking duck and, especially, with the steak and onions Cantonese style. (I think these wines should be guzzled within six or seven years of birth—chased with aspirin and milk thistle . . . the alcohol tops 17 percent.) The 1990 Kreydenweiss Riesling SGN was a sweet finish, though I don't remember it all that well. Two guests were lost for hours in Chinatown after that. Myself and my chef friend Mario Batali went on a tear through the West Village, which was terminated in the wee hours when my girlfriend called with threats and promises. I still don't know what happened to a box of Riedel glasses or to my birthday presents. A good time was had by all.

Asher, Gerald. *On Wine*. New York: Vintage, 1984.

———. *The Pleasures of Wine*. San Francisco: Chronicle Books, 2002.

———. *Vineyard Tales: Reflections on Wine*. San Francisco: Chronicle Books, 1997.

Bastianich, Joseph, and David Lynch. *Vino Italiano: The Regional Wines of Italy*. New York: Clarkson Potter, 2002.

Broadbent, Michael. *The Great Vintage Wine Book II*. London: Christie's, 1991.

———. *Vintage Wine*. New York: Harcourt, 2002.

Clarke, Oz. *New Wine Atlas*. New York: Harcourt, 2002.

Coates, Clive. *Côte d'Or: A Celebration of the Great Wines of Burgundy*. Berkeley: University of California Press, 1997.

———. *The Wines of Bordeaux*. Berkeley: University of California Press, 2004.

Dibdin, Michael. *A Long Finish: An Aurelio Zen Mystery*. New York: Pantheon, 1998.

Duijker, Hubrecht, and Michael Broadbent. *The Bordeaux Atlas and Encyclopaedia of Châteaux*. New York: St. Martin's, 1997.

Duijker, Hubrecht, and Hugh Johnson. *The Wine Atlas of France*. 4th ed. London: Mitchell Beazley, 1997.

Friedrich, Jacqueline. *A Wine and Food Guide to the Loire*. New York: Henry Holt, 1996.

Gambero Rosso. Editore. (Also *Italian Wines 2000*, 2001, 2002, 2003, 2004, 2005.) New York: Gambero Rosso Inc., 2000, 2001, 2002, 2004, 2005.

Haeger, John Winthrop. *North American Pinot Noir*. Berkeley: University of California Press, 2004.

Jefford, Andrew. *The New France*. London: Mitchell Beazley, 2002.

Johnson, Hugh, and James Halliday. *The Vintner's Art*. New York: Simon and Schuster, 1992.

Kramer, Matt. *Making Sense of Burgundy*. New York: William Morrow, 1990.

———. *New California Wine*. Philadelphia: Running Press, 2004.

Lapsley, James T. *Bottled Poetry: Napa Winemaking from Prohibition to the Modern Era*. Berkeley: University of California Press, 1996.

Liebling, A. J. *Between Meals*. New York: Farrar, Straus and Giroux, 1959.

Lukacs, Paul. *American Vintage*. New York: Houghton Mifflin, 2000.

Lynch, Kermit. *Adventures on the Wine Route: A Wine Buyer's Tour of France*. New York: Farrar, Straus and Giroux, 1988.

Markham, Dewey, Jr. *1855: A History of the Bordeaux Classification*. New York: John Wiley, 1998.

Matthews, Patrick. *The Wild Bunch: Great Wines from Small Producers*. London: Faber and Faber, 1997.

McCarthy, Ed, and Mary Ewing-Mulligan. *Champagne for Dummies*. Foster City: IDG Worldwide, 1999.

———. *Wine for Dummies*. 2nd ed. Foster City: IDG Worldwide, 1998.

McCoy, Elin. *The Emperor of Wine*. New York: Ecco, 2005.

Olney, Richard. *French Wine and Food*. Northampton, Mass.: Interlink Publishing Group, 1997.

———. *Reflexions*. New York: Brick Tower Press, 2000.

Parker, Robert, Jr. *Bordeaux: A Comprehensive Guide to the Wines Produced from 1961 to 1997*. New York: Simon and Schuster, 1998.

———. *Bordeaux: A Consumer's Guide to the World's Finest Wines*. New York: Simon and Schuster, 2003.

———. *Wines of the Rhône Valley*. Revised and expanded ed., New York: Simon and Schuster, 1997.

Peynaud, Émile. *The Taste of Wine: The Art and Science of Wine Appreciation*. 2nd ed. Translated by Michael Schuster. New York: John Wiley and Sons, 1996.

Pickett, Rex. *Sideways*. New York: St. Martin's Press, 2004.

Pitiot, Sylvain, and Jean Charles Servant. *Les Vins de Bourgogne*. Paris: Presse Universitaires de France, 1997.

Radford, John. *The Wines of Rioja*. London: Mitchell Beazley, 2004.

Rosen, Jennifer. *Waiter, There's a Horse in My Wine*. Colorado: Dauphin Press, 2005.

Robinson, Jancis, ed. *The Oxford Companion to Wine*. New York: Oxford, 1994.

————. *Vintage Timecharts*. New York: Weidenfeld and Nicolson, 1989.

Steinberg, Edward. *The Making of a Great Wine: Gaja and Sori San Lorenzo*. New York: Ecco, 1992.

Stevenson, Tom. *Christie's World Encyclopedia of Champagne and Sparkling Wine*. London: Wine Appreciation Guild, 1999.

St. Pierre, Brian. *A Perfect Glass of Wine*. San Francisco: Chronicle Books, 1996.

Waugh, Auberon. *Waugh on Wine*. London, 1987.

Wildman, Frederick S., Jr. *A Wine Tour of France*. New York: William Morrow, 1972.

A NOTE ON THE TYPE

This book was set in a version of the well-known Monotype face Bembo. This letter was cut for the celebrated Venetian printer Aldus Manutius by Francesco Griffo, and first used in Pietro Cardinal Bembo's *De Aetna* of 1495. The companion italic is an adaptation of the chancery script type designed by the calligrapher and printer Lodovico degli Arrighi.

Composed by Creative Graphics, Allentown, Pennsylvania

Printed and bound by R.R. Donnelley, Harrisonburg, Virginia

Designed by M. Kristen Bearse